T0094546

"This highly readable, extraordinarily informative and practical guide by Lama Tsomo, an American female lama, is sprinkled with detailed and specific instructions in Tibetan Buddhist meditation practices and with concrete suggestions for promoting happiness and well-being."

—RICHARD J. DAVIDSON, Founder, Center for Healthy Minds, University of Wisconsin—Madison

"In today's fast-paced, high-tech world, the struggle to find truth and meaning requires a special kind of teacher. Thank goodness for the arrival of Lama Tsomo, whose insights and instruction could not have come at a better time."

—VAN JONES, CEO of REFORM Alliance, Host of Redemption Project and the Van Jones Show on CNN

"Before Lama Tsomo, I felt meditation was only in the mind. Through these practices, I felt it come into my heart. Through Lama Tsomo, I found more freedom, laughter and grace. I honor her as a teacher and am grateful she has brought these ideas into a format that is accessible to more people."

—MARIANNE MANILOV, student of Lama Tsomo; founder, Engage Network

"Lama Tsomo's conversational style and clarity, open-mindedness yet dedication all contribute to a book that will meet the needs of a great many who seek to deepen their inner life but are unsure how."

—ARTHUR ZAJONC, Past President of Mind and Life Institute

"Designed for readers from all backgrounds and levels of experience, this beautiful book offers step-by-step guidance in accessible practices, as well as a rich array of stories, scientific perspectives and ways of dealing with challenges that arise on the path. You will find in these pages a precious invitation to inhabit the happiness, love and freedom of your own awakened heart."

—TARA BRACH, PhD, author of *Radical Acceptance* and *True Refuge*

"Especially timely now, when there is so much need for spiritual remedy in this age of increasing inner emptiness in the midst of excessive materialism imbued with collective neurosis."

—ANAM THUBTEN, author of *No Self, No Problem*

"Especially geared for North American wisdom seekers and written in friendly and understandable language, the book serves up a rich feast of abundant and clearly explained practices. Given the perilousness of our times, Lama Tsomo offers an exciting and needed gift of deeper soul journeying into an inner peace and joy."

—THE REV. DR. MATTHEW FOX, his most recent books include *Order of the Sacred Earth, Naming the Unnameable: 89 Wonderful and Useful Names for God . . . Including the Unnameable God,* and *The Lotus & The Rose* with Lama Tsomo

TIBETAN BUDDHIST PRACTICE SERIES

Ancient Wisdom
For Our Times

BOOK 1 *Why Bother? An Introduction*

TIBETAN BUDDHIST PRACTICE SERIES

Ancient Wisdom For Our Times

BOOK 1 *Why Bother? An Introduction*

Lama Tsomo

foreword by HIS HOLINESS THE DALAI LAMA XIV

Namchak

Namchak

PUBLISHING

Namchak

PUBLISHING

*The Namchak Foundation supports the study and
practice of the Namchak Lineage of Tibetan Buddhism*

Namchak.org

Copyright © 2021 by Lama Tsomo LLC

All rights reserved. This book may not be reproduced in whole or in part, stored in a retrieval system, or transmitted in any form or by any means— electronic, mechanical, or other—without written permission from the publisher, except by a reviewer, who may quote brief passages in a review.

Cover design: Kate Basart/Union Pageworks
Book design: Mary Ann Casler & Kate Basart/Union Pageworks
Cover art from *The Encyclopedia of Tibetan Symbols and Motifs* by Robert Beer, © 1999 by Robert Beer. Reprinted by arrangement with Shambhala Publications, Inc., Boulder, CO. www.shambhala.com.
Editorial: Michael Frisbie
Copyeditor: Erin Cusick/Cusick Editing
Indexer: Michael Ferreira/Ferreira Indexing, Inc.
Project and print management: Elizabeth Cromwell/Books in Flight
Printed in Canada

Printed on FSC-certified materials with vegetable-based ink

Library of Congress Control Number: 2020912802

Cataloging-in-Publication data is available from the Library of Congress

ISBN: 978-0-9995770-9-7

First printing, 2021

26 25 24 23 22 21   1 2 3 4 5 6 7 8

Contents

Interestingly, there was no blue light in the room when I took this picture. I know because it was my own kitchen. It only appeared when we developed the film.—Lama Tsomo

Homage

In the Tibetan tradition, I want to begin by paying homage to my Root Lama, Gochen Tulku Sangak* Rinpoche, who has guided me with patience, wisdom, and a good helping of humor, since the beginning of my pursuit of the Vajrayana path. Studying at his feet has been like standing with my mouth open, under a waterfall. As with glaciers flowing to waterfalls, truth and inspiration flow in abundance from the Buddha, through the masters of this lineage, and through Rinpoche. I continue to receive this gift in wonder and gratitude.

---

* Sometimes spelled *Sang-ngag.*

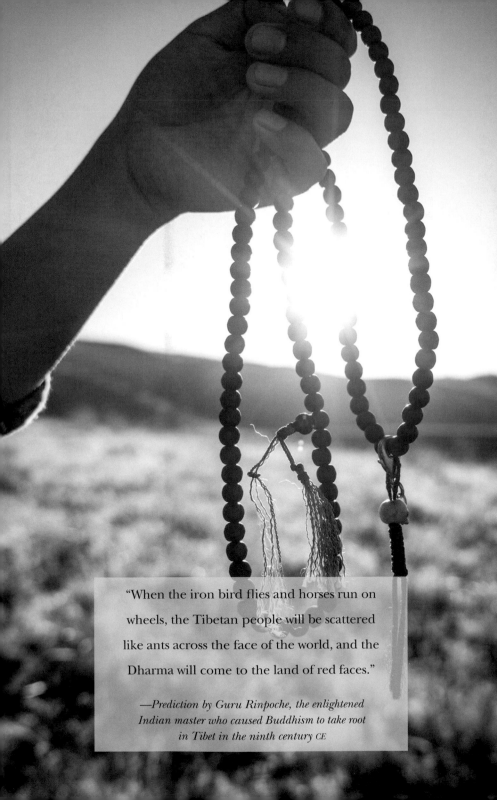

"When the iron bird flies and horses run on wheels, the Tibetan people will be scattered like ants across the face of the world, and the Dharma will come to the land of red faces."

—*Prediction by Guru Rinpoche, the enlightened Indian master who caused Buddhism to take root in Tibet in the ninth century* CE

Tulku Sangak Rinpoche, His Holiness the Dalai Lama XIV, Lama Tsomo

THE DALAI LAMA

FOREWORD

As our world becomes ever more connected, the world's great spiritual traditions are able to get to know each other better. This provides their followers opportunities to learn from one another and develop a deeper appreciation and respect for each other's teachings, traditions and practices. I, for one, have learned a great deal from the insights of spiritual traditions other than my own.

I often describe myself as a staunch Buddhist. However, I have never felt the urge to propagate Buddhism with the aim of converting others to my point of view. In general, I believe it's better and safer for most people to stay within the religious tradition of their birth. The world's faiths evolved in specific geographical and cultural circumstances, which gives them an affinity to the spiritual inclinations and needs of specific communities. I am quite open about this, especially when I am asked to speak about Buddhism in the West, where the main spiritual traditions are historically Judeo-Christian.

At the same time, I recognize that, especially in today's interconnected world, there will be individuals who find the approach of traditions other than those to which they were born to be more effective and suited to their own spiritual aspirations. I know many people in the West, in both North America and Europe, who engage in serious study and practice of Buddhist teachings. They find the advice for training the mind presented in the Buddhist teachings to be profoundly beneficial and meaningful. Some such Western Buddhists have been steadfast in their commitment to their Buddhist practice for several decades, demonstrating a deep dedication. It is in this context that I am happy to see the publication of this new book *A Westerner's Introduction and Guide to Tibetan Buddhism.* Written by Sangak Tsomo, a long-time student and practitioner of Tibetan Buddhism, the book outlines the basic views of the Tibetan tradition and examples of some of its practices for the interested modern reader. I am pleased to note that while the author describes her personal journey into Buddhism in some detail, she continues to honor her traditional Jewish heritage.

I have no doubt that Western readers who wish to deepen their understanding of Tibetan Buddhist practices will find much to interest them here, and that members of other faiths, or even those who have none, will enjoy this sincere account of spiritual exploration.

June 6, 2014

Pema Khandro Ling
1221 Luisa Street, Suite A
Santa Fe, NM 87505
santafe@ewam.org

Ewam Sang-ngag Ling
PO Box 330 Arlee, MT 59821
406.726.0217 • www.ewam.org
admin@ewam.org

Nyingma School of Tibetan Buddhism

Gochen Tulku Sang-ngag Rinpoche
Spiritual Director

Foreword

For the benefit of Westerners who are beginners in the practice of Buddhism, Lama Tsomo has drawn on her own knowledge of Western and Eastern ways of thinking and devoted all her efforts to writing this current work, in order to provide a bridge that will forge a connection between these cultures. I am delighted that she has completed this book, and offer my sincere and heartfelt thanks and best wishes to her in this endeavor.

On this note, let me say a few words about Lama Tsomo, the author of this book, since she is a personal student of mine. Beginning with our initial meeting in 1995, she undertook the study and practice of the Buddhist teachings, including her spending two or three months each year in strict retreat, in addition to maintaining an uninterrupted daily practice. In this way, she has dedicated herself enthusiastically to completing a system of training from the preliminary stages up to and including the advanced yogic disciplines (*tsa-lung*) and Dzogchen practices.

On the basis of her efforts, in 2005 I formally recognized Lama Tsomo's accomplishments in an investiture ceremony that took place in conjunction with the graduation of the nuns who participated in the three-year retreat program at my meditation center of Kusum Khandro Ling in Pharping, Nepal.

Following this, in 2006, on the occasion of the final year of the intensive study program at Ewam Sang-ngag Ling in Arlee, Montana, I conferred on Lama Tsomo the formal title of a lama of the Ewam Foundation.

She has now authored this book to introduce people to the Buddhist teachings, in order to help new practitioners on into the future. I encourage all to read and study this text with a sense of trust in its usefulness, and am sure that they will profit greatly through such efforts. Please take this advice to heart.

This was written in my retreat cabin by the teaching throne of Longchenpa at Ewam Pema Khandro Ling, by me, the sixth holder of the title of Gochen Tulku.

Sang-ngag Tenzin
April 2014

~ *Ewam Nepal* ~
Turquoise Leaf Nunnery - Phone: 977-1-710-094/Sang-ngag Phurba Ling Retreat Center - Phone: 977-1-710-093
POB 7032 Devi G.B.S. Pharping Kathmandu, Nepal

Ewam is a federally registered 501(c)(3) US non-profit organization

WHO IS LAMA TSOMO?
And Why Should I Listen to Her?

As you read this book, and others in the series, you will come to know Lama Tsomo well: not just her teachings, but her "story"—the personal and spiritual path that led her to this book, and to you.

Before you begin, though, you may be curious about her credentials. Lama Tsomo has spent a total of three years of strict, solitary retreat under the guidance of Tulku Sangak Rinpoche, during which time she progressed through all the stages of the Vajrayana path, the branch of Buddhism practiced in Tibet. In addition she has undergone thirty 1- to 2-week-long intensive trainings with Tulku Sangak Rinpoche and Khen Rinpoche. In 2005, Tulku Sangak Rinpoche ordained her as a lama in the Namchak tradition.

For a more thorough Curriculum Vitae please turn to page 127.

—*Editor*

Yet, smile he does. Constantly, joyfully. Hour after hour, year after year, no matter what happens. Although he is unquestionably a heavy-weight scholar and master practitioner, his constant joyfulness is palpable. His infectious laugh rolls out at the slightest provocation, and he jokes quite a bit, himself . . . then laughs at his own jokes!

This is not because he forgets the plight of his people, or sweeps his own suffering under the rug. When a nun, Ani Tenzin Palmo, spoke to him about the plight of women who had been trying to devote their lives to the *Dharma* with almost no support from the lamas, His Holiness burst into tears on the spot. He resolved that far greater opportunities had to be provided for women to reach the heights of scholarship and practice that men had been supported in pursuing.

Meanwhile, the sun came out shortly after that, and he was smiling again . . . while not forgetting his resolution. He has indeed—of course—followed through, and despite the challenge of changing age-old culture quickly, much progress has been made since then.

If you were to ask His Holiness why he smiles, of course I can't predict what he'd say. But judging from his writings and from witnessing him personally many times, I would say this:

He has plumbed the depths of understanding the nature of the universe and the nature of the mind. He has trained his own mind—

both brain and heart. He has concluded that we are not separate from each other, as we so persistently think we are. I believe he lives within a view that holds the truth of our common root of being. He sees this as an ongoing reality, and stands in that reality.

Compassion, then, comes quite naturally if a person lives from that reality. And so does joy. He doesn't have to busy himself with "looking out for number one." (Or, to put it another way, the "one" he is looking out for is the "one" that is, ultimately, all of us.) Imagine that. What a *relief!* What *freedom.*

Every day, he spends several hours in our universal "home"—that great ocean of compassionate awareness that I've spoken of. After his morning meditation, he sees with a clean lens everywhere he looks, so he perceives something close to the exquisitely beautiful *pureland* (heavenly realm) and pure inhabitants that are the true nature of things. Everything around him is alive. He sees each of us as another beautiful wave in the constant "dis*play*" of that great ocean. He sees the relatively tiny significance of his own wave-existence.

And remember, within and throughout that whole ocean . . . is *joy.* The kind we never have to depart from, even at death.

The Buddha has invited us home and shown us the way. Won't you come along?

preferred. Almost every day I would stand in the lunchroom with my tray, looking at each of the tables with each of the cliques, wondering who I would sit with that day. Would it be Carla, who was sitting with the uncool artist clique? Or Jane, who was with her clique—the class brains/geeks? Or Becca, who was in the almost-in group? I slid through it all, hardly noticed. That would include boys. I had almost no dates. I wasn't the type to want to go to parties and be "in." I had enough friends to be content with my social life, other than wishing for a boyfriend, of course.

My childhood had been a depressing experience for me. I had grown up in a family that had all its physical requirements taken care of, but not all our emotional needs. I felt close to my father, but he had to travel constantly for his work and, even when in town, worked long hours at the office.

Children, especially young children, need their parents to be perfect and godlike, and even as we grow up, we may expect parental perfection. My parents were good-hearted but neurotic human beings, trying their best, just like all the rest of us. They each blessed me with wonderful gifts, but they also committed sins of omission and commission. I grew up a neurotic mere human as well, and raised my own children imperfectly—guaranteed.

As children, we all suffer from that huge divide between what we want/need and what our very human parents can give. As I was growing up, I suffered from that too, in many ways.

Throughout my childhood I felt lonely, sad, and not very safe. I used to cry for no apparent reason, and I was just waiting to graduate high school and leave home. The underlying tone of that time was a melancholic longing, though I didn't even know for *what*.

These circumstances—the suffering in and around me, these gaps, my sense of not being connected—motivated me to search, though at first I wasn't really sure what I was searching *for* to ease my loneliness and longing.

I remember riding on the bus one day in junior high, thinking, "If I could just not feel the bad feelings and only feel the good ones, wouldn't that be great?" In my effort not to feel the loneliness, pain, and frustration in my life, I gradually went numb. Unfortunately that numbness didn't allow me to feel any of life, even the joyful moments. Though I didn't understand it at the time, I was depressed. One somewhat bright spot in my day was eating. Consequently I did too much of it.

When I was fifteen, I went on a camping trip across the country, which changed my life. We lived outside for two months, in some of the most spectacular national parks this land has to offer. I came to a deep sense of humans in relation to the natural world . . . on *its* terms. When I returned to our apartment in the city, I realized that modern

After the empowerment, I came for a personal interview with Rinpoche. Since he didn't know a word of English, and at the time I didn't know a word of Tibetan, we needed a translator. It just happened to be Sangye Khandro, a leading translator in the West, who had almost never translated for Rinpoche.

Rinpoche was medium height and wiry, with dark, weathered skin. Somehow the patterns of his wrinkles made beautiful designs. He seemed middle-aged, but it was impossible to tell how old he really was. When he smiled, he showed big white teeth, and the weathered skin crinkled around his eyes in the most appealing shapes. His smiles were infectious. Luckily they came almost constantly, in waves, sometimes tiny, sometimes huge, accompanied by a surprisingly high-pitched laugh that tickled me from the inside so that I had to laugh too. And this was before the translation of what he said.

Contrary to many Western notions about enlightened Asian masters, Rinpoche hardly stayed still. Sometimes he doodled with a pencil and paper while waiting for the translations back and forth. Sometimes he lightly jumped up and paced around the room. Wherever he went, he left trails of graceful line drawings of lotuses, clouds, calligraphy, and other images. His fine-boned hands made the most lovely gestures that had a grace about them that wasn't at all like Western men's, yet wasn't in the least effeminate. His voice was low and kind of froggy, occasionally leaping into falsetto to emphasize a

THIS PAGE: *Tulku Sangak Rinpoche, presiding over the monthlong blessing of the Garden of One Thousand Buddhas.*
PAGES 26–27: *Ewam Sangha members and friends, enjoying a ceremonial feast during the monthlong blessing of the Garden of One Thousand Buddhas.*

word here or there. I've since noticed that the Dalai Lama and many other Tibetan men use this falsetto for emphasis as well.

I thought of a question for which I wanted a clear, definitive answer. Many, if not most, of the Buddhists in the world are vegetarian. If Tibetans are devout Buddhists, with compassion for *all* beings, why do most of them eat meat? I was eating mostly vegetarian at the time, and was a lifelong animal lover, so it was important to me, and I couldn't make sense of this. What about the karma involved for the one eating the meat?

I put the question to him. He said, "If we actually kill an animal ourselves, it holds the most serious karmic consequences for us. It's murder, of course. If we do this repeatedly, we develop a habit of killing, which will follow us, along with the karmic seeds, into future lives. The next worst thing is if we choose a particular animal and ask that it be killed for us to eat." At that point I thought of restaurants that offer to kill the lobster of your choice from a huge aquarium. I could see his points for both of these examples. Then he went on. "It's much better if we just go to the store and pick up any package of meat and buy it." That didn't make much sense to me.

"Wait, but how does that work karmically, Rinpoche? We're still paying money that goes back to the butcher who did the killing. It's indirect, but it still gets there. This encourages him and other butchers to keep on killing animals for a living. We're voting with our dollars for the killing of animals. In America we have laws against paying someone else to kill a person for us. Isn't this a close relative of that? True, we haven't chosen a specific animal, but aren't we stepping into other, additional karmic territory when we encourage someone else to murder by paying them to do so? And by the way, what about the karma we now have with the butchers?"

After some back-and-forth on this point, Rinpoche said, "Of course, the very best is to give up meat altogether. A few great masters in exile don't eat meat, and they don't allow their students to either. Another practice we traditionally do in Tibet, to make the situation a little better, is to wait until the butcher has offered the meat to two other people. The thought is that if the animal has already died, then we're simply eating the meat before the bugs get it." He and I came to agreement that not eating meat was optimal, but barring that, the more distance between the eater and the killing, the better.

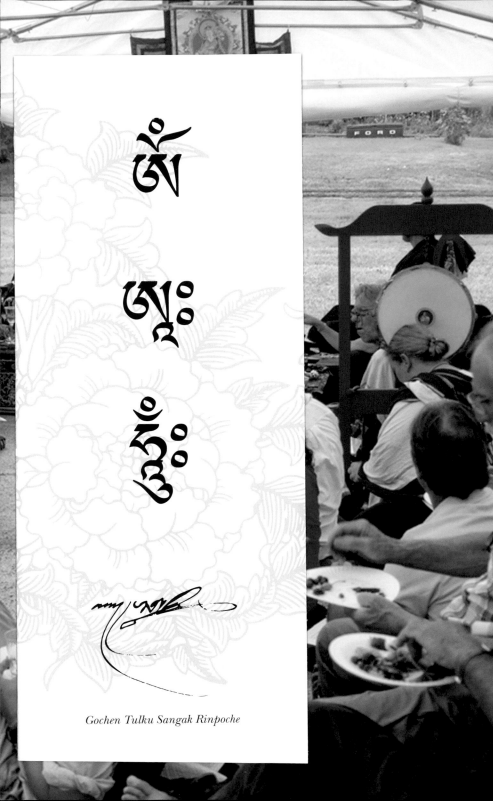

ༀ

ཨཱཿ

ཧཱུྃ

Gochen Tulku Sangak Rinpoche

Our short, lively discussion took a few loops and bends along its course, but essentially that was what we discussed in the landmark interview. Then it was over. I didn't think much about it, except for some more about Tibetans and meat. For example, since they live in a very extreme and challenging environment, and almost the only things that grow there are trees (mostly conifers) and grass, they don't have a lot of dietary options. Their only real options are to eat the grass and the grass-eaters. Toasted barley flour is a staple there, so that would be a small part of the grass. But without four stomachs, they wouldn't be able to get all their nutrition from grass, especially for withstanding the rigors of the high Himalayas; and this without indoor heat. As a practical matter, how could such an environment support a human population if they didn't eat the grass-eaters?

Shortly after that conversation, I had to give up vegetarianism because of increasingly serious health problems. I still don't feel fully resolved on this issue, even though His Holiness the Dalai Lama has also had to go back to eating meat.

In all of this pondering, the most obvious, striking point never occurred to me. This lama, who had just dropped in from nowhere to this out-of-the-way place, happened to be giving a lineage transmission and introduction to the very next practice I was about to start doing . . . *and I didn't get that he was the teacher I'd been praying for!*

SECOND MEETING: RECOGNITION

The next time I saw Rinpoche he came to my *house*. For two weeks. With one of the world's best translators, Chökyi Nyima (Richard Barron), who at the time never did that sort of event.

Yes, I did finally get a clue, but slowly.

We *thought* that Rinpoche was coming because Sherab no longer lived at the house near Santa Fe and needed to get some teachings from Rinpoche. At the time Sherab was staying in a cramped apartment with two other people. Would I mind hosting him, Rinpoche, and Chökyi while he got *Dzogchen* teachings, the highest in Rinpoche's path, for a couple of weeks? Sure, why not?

Another sign I had totally missed at the time was from a dinner I'd had two years earlier with Ram Dass. I was a longtime fan, and I'd asked him which meditation might be best for me to pursue. He uttered one strange word: *Dzogchen*. Now, here was Sherab coming to my home to study Dzogchen from one of the world's foremost Dzogchen lamas, and I'd totally forgotten Ram Dass's advice!

Sherab said I could sit in on the teachings. This didn't make sense to me. I was doing Ngöndro, the very beginning stage of Vajrayana; Dzogchen was the very highest level. Why would I plop down into these high-level teachings at this point? Sherab kept assuring me it didn't matter, but I wasn't convinced. It seemed to me that it could cause problems for me and the others there.

As the time drew closer, I became more concerned. Then something else happened. I found out that Sherab had been turning other people away from this teaching, telling them that *I* had pronounced it a "closed retreat." This seemed totally against the order of things. Wouldn't that be up to the lama doing the teaching? The other issue was that, well, Sherab had just made that up. Since he had told me that for Dzogchen teachings, the connections between participants had to be utterly clean, I became really concerned about the convergence of these issues leading up to the retreat. I called Rinpoche. Fortunately Chökyi, the translator, "happened" to be on hand. Through him, I expressed my concerns to Rinpoche about both the appropriateness of my sitting in and Sherab's telling people that I'd declared it a closed retreat. I felt that both matters were up to Rinpoche as the teacher.

Rinpoche said that he saw my concern as a very good sign, and that I was right to call. He went on to say that the heart of the matter was my motivation, and he could see that my motivation was pure. For that reason, he knew that everything would play out well. He would start by

giving some Ngöndro teachings; then we would just see how it went. That was all he expressed, yet somehow I hung up with all of my concerns laid to rest. I felt happy and ready for the retreat.

Just before he arrived, Sherab gave me a little advice. He said, "I know you love to ask questions and hammer out points. Your questions and thinking are all great, and I really appreciate it, but this is a rinpoche—a high lama. Tibetans find it disrespectful to ask a lot of questions."

"Really?" I exclaimed, recalling the questions I had showered Rinpoche with and our lively debate during our first meeting. What he was saying didn't fit with my experience of Rinpoche. Besides, there was a practical need here. "But . . . what if I need to know the *answer*?"

"Just don't ask too many questions."

I found this to be an impossible conundrum. "But how will I find out the answer? Why is he coming here if I can't find things out from him? What's disrespectful about asking a question?" I asked, my questions coming out in a torrent. His admonition to ask no questions only stimulated more questions!

The first day we opened with a *tsok*, or gathering. This ceremonial feast usually lasts about two hours and involves a constant stream of melodious chanting in Tibetan, punctuated by drums and bells. Every so often Sherab, who was assisting, would walk in or out, carrying symbolic cakes that had been sculpted into inscrutable shapes. Luckily, toward the end we got to stop and eat the food that had been offered and blessed during the ceremony. We could have a bit of conversation, thanks to the translator. Then there were concluding prayers to finish it off.

Since at that time I knew absolutely no Tibetan, nor anything about such ceremonies, I was at a loss. Fortunately, the constant chant was a beautiful, intricate melody. It was sometimes alternated with another, simpler one. As one looking at the prospect of becoming a Vajrayana practitioner, I wasn't sure how I would do with all the pomp and circumstance. I'd been drawn to Vajrayana by the effective mind-training methods. I didn't see what all this two-hour ceremony had to do with that.

It was years before I learned that it was all a group meditation, guided by the liturgy, with visualizations that, in refined archetypal language, honored the land guardians, brought forth various aspects of my own Buddha Nature, made extensive use of archetypes, and worked with emotions and energies in highly refined ways. When I say "highly refined," I mean that these methods of guiding the mind to a more enlightened state have been developed and distilled over thousands of years, with millions of people, to achieve their desired effect. The process, if done consciously, can be quite powerful, with surprising effects. Who knew?

At last we settled down for the first session of teachings. According to plan, Rinpoche held forth on the first stages of the Ngöndro, or Preliminary Practices, which I had already gotten a good start on. He was constantly bringing forth fascinating and profound levels of understanding.

These understandings rang true for me.

I was writing notes furiously. After he had held forth on the "*bodhicitta* training" section for a while, he opened it up for questions. I looked at Sherab. He gave a slight nod. I was at least permitted one question.

"Rinpoche, you've just told us that in practicing the highest form of bodhicitta, we put others' needs before ours, like a shepherd. But you've also said we need to become enlightened first before we can really help sentient beings to break free of Samsara [potentially endless cycle of rebirth]. Aren't there times when it's like the oxygen mask on an airplane? Parents are told to put their *own* mask on first, not out of self-interest, but *so that* they can best help their child. What are

we to do in the case of enlightenment ourselves? When do we work to directly benefit others, and when do we work directly on our own minds, even if the ultimate altruistic goal is the same?"

Rinpoche seemed to wake up, and leaned forward. He talked in a very energetic, animated way for some time. Here's the gist of what Chökyi translated: We do need to pursue enlightenment in order to be of any use in helping other Samsaric beings. How can we help a drowning person if we can't swim ourselves? (This made sense to me. When I studied Junior Lifeguarding, the instructors began with that very point, and trained us accordingly.) We pursue our own enlighten-ment *in order* to help others. This is why in Mahayana, or Great Vehicle, Buddhism, we begin all of our practice sessions, ceremonies, and teach-ings by arousing bodhicitta.* We bring forward in our minds what's known as the Two Purposes: enlightenment for self and others. We're doing this practice on behalf of all sentient beings, even in the Dharma activity, such as study and practice.

But the benefit continues. Because of the training we do, we're far more masterful at helping others during the course of the day. We're less likely to fall into anger, protect our own projects at the expense of others, get distracted, and so on. If we carry this desire to serve others on their path of enlightenment (whether they're consciously pursuing it or not), we then bring forth our own Buddha Nature, which in turn serves to help our own enlightenment process. This then translates into clearer seeing (through a cleaner windshield) and better medi-tation. These support each other, and everyone, you and they, moves forward, just as a shepherd moves forward with the flock. He contin-ued leaning forward, clearly fully engaged. He was having fun; I was sure of it. For all I could tell, he liked answering questions *best of all.* "Do you have any more questions?" he queried.

It just so happened I did. I'd been writing them in the margins as Rinpoche was going along. But I had a different question I had to ask first, to clear the air. "I've been told that asking questions of a high lama such as you is disrespectful. Is that true?"

---

* In Sanskrit, *bodhicitta* means "heart/mind of awakening." This awakened heart/ mind feels our connection to all beings, and therefore, their joy and pain.

Tulku Sangak Rinpoche, Namchak Khen Rinpoche, and others, circumambulating the Garden of One Thousand Buddhas. Circumambulation is said to help us to absorb the blessings of enlightened mind, in pilgrimage spots such as this.

*Tulku Sangak Rinpoche, presiding over the consecration ceremony
of the Stupa Garden at the Namchak Retreat Ranch*

to tap us from behind and win his point. Every once in a while we'd
have him cornered, and it was time for him to admit we were right. But
his pride wouldn't quite allow him to give in to his kids. So we had no
choice: an all-out napkin fight would ensue, fairly athletic, accompanied by raucous laughter. Mom would cover her face, warning, "Look
out for my contact lenses! My contacts, my contacts!" This was often
the grand finale to our dinners.

Needless to say, I was ready for the debate with Rinpoche. I have
no idea if my points were worth anything in the Dzogchen context,
but Rinpoche and I were off and running. We were having a grand
time, and I was learning a mile a minute. Alas, not having had the
benefit of my childhood dinner table, Sherab sat mute. I was letting it all hang out: my ignorance and knowledge, and of course
my enthusiasm for the topic. Sherab seemed to be holding it all in.

I couldn't tell what was happening inside my dear friend. Was he horrified at my uppitiness? Surprised at the whole turn of events? Frustrated that he couldn't jump in? Surely he wasn't lost . . . or was he? I just couldn't read his unmoving face. Afterward I felt concerned for him.

Later I heard him teaching his little *Sangha* (spiritual community) in the Bay Area, beautifully weaving in the Dzogchen understandings Rinpoche had brought us. Everything had no doubt registered, but both his culture and his own personality were vastly different from mine. My personality and cultural tendencies certainly limit me in some frustrating ways, but I was sad that Sherab's own tendencies didn't allow Rinpoche to see how much he'd understood after all. They never did connect very strongly, probably because of destiny as much as anything else, and Sherab has since moved on.

Back at the seminal Dzogchen retreat, the teachings progressed apace. One night Chökyi left to visit some friends. Sherab withdrew to his room for the duration.

When Chökyi walked out, the translation door instantly slammed shut. We didn't have a word in common. My teenage daughter Anna, Rinpoche, and I looked at each other. Now what? Rinpoche got the goofiest look on his face, plopped a hat on at a crazy angle, and pranced around, laughing his high-pitched laugh. He was totally *silly*. Anna and I cracked up. I grabbed Sherab's size 14 wide shoes and clomped around, my toothpick ankles looking particularly ridiculous sticking out of them. Rinpoche threw his head back, laughing. Then we were arm wrestling. Then an uproarious tickle fight.

Later, Rinpoche watched, fascinated, as I cooked up our dinner. Between prison and monasteries, I guessed that he'd never learned to cook a thing. The next morning I found this to be true. He sheepishly asked me to show him how to light the stove burner so he could make his early-morning tea.

It also occurred to Anna and me that as a *tulku* (high, reincarnated lama), maybe he'd rarely had this kind of silly, irreverent, slapstick interaction with people. This turned out to be mostly true as well, except for some times, especially earlier in his life, when he was with fellow tulkus. As the head of a lineage, now mostly presiding over his own monastery, he didn't get the chance often. That night the time flew by as we all partied down.

A different kind of bonding can happen outside the teaching arena—beyond words as well. I learned still more about Rinpoche that evening. His obsession for learning, whether fine points about a Dharma text or how a gas stove works, knows no bounds. You can be sure he'll spend time contemplating the inscrutable English writing (Light, Off, Hi, Lo) on the knobs. He doesn't identify with one persona or another. He's equally believable, equally comfortable— equally himself—whether wearing the lineage lama crown while teaching thousands of devout followers, or losing an arm-wrestling match and collapsing into falsetto giggles. He never forgets his true essence, which can take any form.

Toward the end of the teachings, I began asking him questions about my college epiphany that no one had been able to explain. I can't go into detail here, because you would first need to have had

Dzogchen empowerments and teachings. Much of the Dzogchen knowledge is closely guarded, partly so that the practitioner hears the teachings freshly when their mind has been made thoroughly ready. Then they can fall into seeing/experiencing things as they naturally are. What I want to tell you and *can* tell you here is that when I heard his answers, they instantly rang true. This was the first time in my life that had happened.

I didn't register it consciously at the moment, but I had already come to know that he was my lama.

At that time, I was in the editing phase of a book I'd written, which included traditional stories of feminine journeys, with female protagonists displaying distinctly feminine strengths. Instead of killing dragons to save their beloveds, they wielded the power of loving connection, endurance, and other feminine traits. I wanted both boys and girls to be fed these images so that they would have those models to follow in their own lives. A central thought of mine was that we all need to balance the masculine and feminine principles, using the best of both.

One night during the retreat, Rinpoche mentioned that he was doing research for a book he wanted to write on female *mahasiddhas*— highly realized beings. He wanted to provide models for Tibetans, especially women, so they would believe that they too could reach enlightenment. Imagine my surprise and delight! Later in the conversation, he mentioned that he wanted to call his new nonprofit *Ewam,* a Sanskrit word meaning "the union of the realized masculine and feminine principles." At that moment there was a ratification in my head, confirming what I'd already come to know. Inside, in celebration of the obvious, I rejoiced, "This is the lama for me!"

As we waited together for his plane, he played with the turquoise *mala* (Tibetan rosary) he'd been fiddling with almost constantly throughout the teachings. This was the mala that he'd been praying with and handling during his waking hours, for the year since Sherab had given it to him. As he tossed it lightly back and forth between his hands, I had this odd idea that he was going to give it to me. I thought, "Oh, how conceited!" They announced that it was time to board. Suddenly, deliberately, he pressed the mala into my hand and lightly skipped off to the plane. I stood there, stunned. After some time my legs moved, but I was still stunned.

A central relationship had begun, the likes of which I'd never heard about, much less experienced. It was more profound and intimate than a romantic one, more enduring than familial ones in some ways, more primary in some ways than any I'd known. It took time to develop fully—in this lifetime, anyway—but develop it did. This sort of experience was hardly a novelty in Asia, but to me it was entirely uncharted territory of the heart.

As Rinpoche knew from the beginning and I came to know much later, our relationship had begun lifetimes ago, and will no doubt go on into future ones. Who knows how many times he's patiently shown me the nature of my mind, of reality, and the relationship between the two? To this day our connection continually deepens. And as my capacity of mind has grown, I've been able to see Rinpoche's vast, wise mind more and more fully. As a natural result, my love for and devotion to him have grown even richer and more profound.

When I first had teachings from Rinpoche, he was the only one in all my life who could thoroughly explain to me, in a way that rang true, all that I'd seen in that epiphany so long ago. He has since gone on to teach me methods that can bring that same level of seeing and more, every time I meditate! Even in between. Not only that, I'm far happier, ongoing, than I was before.

It didn't happen overnight, and it didn't happen without effort. I'm also definitely not finished yet, though it's been nearly two decades and I've spent two to three months out of most of those years in solitary, strict practice retreat. How realistic is it to expect enlightenment in ten easy lessons? If we've been wandering around Samsara for endless lifetimes since beginningless time*, getting all the more ingrained and entangled in wrong ways of seeing and doing, it's going to take a little while to turn ourselves around.

---

* If time is eternal, then there's no beginning.

Tulku Sangak Rinpoche's brother, Namchak Khen Ngawang Gelek
Rinpoche, with Lama Tsomo at the Garden of One Thousand Buddhas.
Khen Rinpoche teaches at both Ewam and Namchak.

Fortunately this path has its rewards along the way—some lofty, some more mundane. On a very practical level, right after I'd had those first teachings with Rinpoche, I was able to give up smoking . . . *through lack of interest!* Have you ever heard of that? I hadn't. Because he'd helped me connect so well with the practices, they were so satisfying on every level—even a gut level—that I actually forgot to smoke.

There was much I'd turned to—taken refuge in—that I was gradually able to loosen my grip on as I went along, including angry words and behavior. I'm not perfect, but I'm much improved and much happier. As I've said, the level of awareness I can reach in my daily meditation meets and can even surpass my first epiphany. For now, I'll take that.

short and direct one. Still, as with many smaller lineages, it's within the larger Nyingma Lineage.

One day when Tulku Sangak Rinpoche was just old enough to run around—still a toddler—he was playing on the hillside with his little friends. The weather was warm, and they were barefoot. As they were running up the hill, he found he could easily sink his foot into the bare rock, leaving a clear imprint, as though it were soft mud. Actually the rock was particularly hard in that area. The other children noticed the imprint and drew their breath in amazement. They ran to tell the adults nearby. Everyone whispered that this must be a great reincarnated lama—a *tulku!*

As word quickly spread, a woman from another lineage became unhappy. When she thought no one was looking, she went to that hillside and tried to chisel out the clear footprint. The stone was so hard that after hours of work she had managed to chisel only two tiny places from the middle of the imprint. She became nervous, gave up the pursuit, and left. Of course, in such a small community, everyone found out about her efforts.

As you can see from the image on the preceding page, the imprint of the little toes is very clear, as is the heel. In the middle are the two little black holes that the lady managed to chisel out.

When Tulku Sangak Rinpoche was about three years old and just barely able to put simple sentences together, his parents told him he would be the keeper of their family lineage. He answered, "No, I'm the tulku of the *Gochen* Monasteries"—a group of monasteries in the Namchak Lineage and in the same province, but not right where they lived. His parents were startled, and not entirely pleased. They wanted him to live in their ancestral home-cum-monastery and take care of the lineage *there*. They quickly hushed him: "Shhh. Don't tell anybody."

Soon after, they were walking down the streets of town and came upon a high lama with the usual sign—an ornamental knob with a tassel hanging from the bridle of his horse. This lama's name was Dzigar Kongtrül Rinpoche. He was another rinpoche, one who had been a dear friend of my lama, Tulku Sangak Rinpoche, in his own previous incarnation. (Since that meeting, Dzigar Kongtrül passed away, then reincarnated himself, and now lives in Colorado. Even in this life he is still called Dzigar Kongtrül Rinpoche.) When these two rinpoches met that day long ago, on that street in Tibet, the tiny Sangak Rinpoche

(my lama) pointed to the ornament and called out, "Hey, that's MINE!" At first Dzigar Kongtrül paid no attention. The tiny Rinpoche insisted louder and louder, saying, "I gave it to you, now give it BACK!" Finally Kongtrül Rinpoche got off his horse and approached the toddler. He looked at him closely, calculated his age, and thought, "He really could be my old friend, the Gochen Tulku, who passed away about four years ago."

Shortly before he died, the Gochen Tulku had given that tassel to his good friend Kongtrül Rinpoche, asking him to keep it until he returned. The lama asked the little boy several questions. Being just under three years old, he forgot his parents' admonishments and answered truthfully. He was, indeed, the Gochen Tulku. Now everyone on the street knew it; there was no hiding it.

His outer circumstances were challenging, to say the least, but it was the firebrand of resentment, burning twenty-four hours a day inside his heart, that he found intolerable.

It was when they moved him to a labor camp and worked him like an ox that he met Tulku Orgyen Chemchok, who had been in permanent retreat in the mountains when the Chinese bound him and brought him to prison. He was working there as a cook.

He asked Rinpoche, "Are you just pretending to do the work while breaking tools or just making a noise when they're not looking?" He was. "Don't you see? In some lifetime, maybe millions of years ago, you planted the karmic seed that has now ripened into this circumstance. If you didn't still have the traces of that previous action in your mindstream [fleck of consciousness that continues through lifetimes], it would be impossible for you to find yourself in this circumstance. Now that you're here, you could simply do the work to be done, and practice while that karmic result exhausts itself, or you could make more negative karma—plant the seeds for future misery—all the while. Then in some lifetime you'll have to live through that result too." Rinpoche could see his point.

"Do you realize that, just as your karmic load is lightening from repaying some karmic debt, the guards are taking on an extremely heavy one? If you think about it, they deserve your sincere compassion." True enough. After all, Rinpoche had studied the law of cause and effect, action and result, known as *karma*. *Karma* is a Sanskrit word, literally meaning "action." We have a corollary in the famous Biblical quote "Ye shall reap what ye sow."

Rinpoche took the tulku's sage advice to heart. He spent every Sunday, when they had a day off from work, helping the tulku, studying, and practicing. He somehow managed to practice a surprising amount in secret, all week. Of course they were forbidden to study Dharma, or even to possess a bit of paper with teachings on it. So the tulku put grease on a flat metal surface, sprinkled sand on it, and wrote crucial bits of the scriptural teachings and practice instructions on the surface. Rinpoche would have to memorize it on the spot; then they would destroy any trace of the writing.

He put the teachings into practice as he did his work, before and after work, at lunch breaks, in any way he could. He tied many knots in a string, and secretly recited mantras while counting on his string like a rosary, under his sleeve. Soon the burning anger was gone from his heart, he had a much more kind and compassionate view toward his captors, and life was becoming tolerable—more than tolerable. Gradually, he was actually beginning to feel contentment. Later, while practicing openly outside Tibet, Rinpoche found that all the scriptures and oral explanations, which the tulku had taught him from memory, had been faultless.

Finally Rinpoche experienced something that changed his heart forever. After he had been in prison for years, Tulku Orgyen Chemchok asked him, "How are you collecting food for the pigs?" The prison kept pigs, which the guards and prisoners ate. The prisoners were required to earn daily "credit" for a certain number of pounds of leaves for the pigs, after a long, hard day's work in the woods. The feed truck would come by, and the prisoners would load their amount onto the scale. Not surprisingly, they mostly loaded big branches, rather than leaves, because branches weighed more and were easier to gather. Rinpoche did the same. The tulku said, "Come with me." He took Rinpoche to the pigpen.

There were the pigs, who were meant to forage in the woods, but instead were cooped up in a pen. They had nothing under their feet but all the sticks left over from their feed, covered with the slime of their own filth. They could hardly walk on that surface. They were

searching desperately through a fresh load of feed for the few leaves they could actually eat. A sharp pang of deep compassion sprang up in Rinpoche's heart. He burst into tears. These pigs were in prison too—one far worse than his. They were just as powerless to escape as he was. Then, of course, there was the fate awaiting them. After their short life in this excruciating pen, they would be killed. He vowed with all his heart to feed them well and to convince his prison friends to do the same. They all agreed, and from then on collected only leaves for the pigs.

This was about much more than a few pigs. Rinpoche's heart had completely turned. He had truly taken the Dharma to heart, and into action, living more purely out of compassion for all beings. Finally, he came to feel truly happy, all of this while still in prison. That firebrand of resentment was extinguished—replaced by peace and joy.

Not coincidentally, he had gone from an inner-hell-realm experience to that of a pure realm (the Tibetan equivalent of heaven), even though his outer circumstances hadn't changed. The Buddha taught that to live from our small sense of self (*ego*, meaning "I" in Latin) is a recipe for misery. To live with a vast sense of Self that includes all sentient beings is a recipe for happiness.

Rinpoche recognized that all the while he was in prison, his karma for that situation was exhausting itself as he followed the tulku's advice and the Buddha's teaching. In his view, it was a sort of work-study program at a monastery with bad food.

Whenever I want to blame outer circumstances, or other people, for my mood, this story helps me put it all in perspective. It also inspires me to have real faith in these methods, with Rinpoche's ability to apply them in "real time" as a sublime example.

After Rinpoche had been in prison for over nine years, Mao Zedong died, the Cultural Revolution along with him. Soon Rinpoche and all the others imprisoned simply for religious leadership were allowed to go.

After he was released, he did a traditional form of traveling retreat for a year. In Lhasa, the capital of Tibet, he met with his lama, Tulku Orgyen Chemchok, who advised him to leave the country. "You need to study with great lamas, and that can't happen here in Tibet now." So with a companion, another tulku, Rinpoche escaped Tibet.

He arrived in Bhutan and studied under the great Dilgo Khyentse (*din*-go *chyent*-sey) Rinpoche for fourteen years. Khyentse Rinpoche was extremely accomplished, and renowned as both a scholar and a meditator. As a young man, he'd meditated in a cave for twelve years and reached an extremely high state of accomplishment as a yogi. He went on to master the scholarly teachings of many lineages, and was the leader of the Tibetan Buddhist Rimey (ecumenical) movement.

For example, Khyentse Rinpoche was the head of the Nyingma Lineage, yet he'd taught and exchanged empowerments with His Holiness the Dalai Lama xiv, head of the Gelugpa Lineage. The Nyingma Lineage is possibly the most populous of the major Tibetan lineages, and Khyentse Rinpoche remained its leader until his passing into Parinirvana (a reverent term for "death") in 1991, leaving behind many relics in his body.

While studying under his constant guidance, Tulku Sangak Rinpoche served Khyentse Rinpoche for the last fourteen years of Khyentse Rinpoche's life, helping to create his temple in exile and train the monks, presiding over the three-year retreat cloister, presiding over the seminary for several years, watching over the monastery when he didn't accompany Khyentse Rinpoche on his many travels, presiding over the monastery for several summer retreats, building stupas (monuments that hold relics[*]), and helping in many other ways.

A few years ago Khyentse Rinpoche's grandson, Rabjam Rinpoche, now running Khyentse Rinpoche's monasteries, asked Tulku Sangak Rinpoche to teach Dzogchen to the highest masters of the monastery, because Tulku Sangak Rinpoche knew better than anyone the system that Khyentse Rinpoche had taught. Tulku Sangak Rinpoche continues these teachings today.

Coming to America

Tulku Sangak Rinpoche first heard of America when he was eight years old. For no apparent reason he was immediately taken with it and thought of nothing else for a week. He told himself, "When I grow up, I'm going to live there."

---

[*]   These can be hair, clothing, or something from a highly realized person. It is believed to carry some of their realization—a truer view of reality.

He had countless visions of America. One was of the land that has become his main center in America, in Arlee, Montana. As we drove around one day, looking for a spot for this center, we thought it would be good to find a piece of land along the main local highway, 93. We wandered onto a sheep ranch, just off the highway, that Rinpoche seemed to respond to immediately. Later he told me he'd recognized that exact view from one of his visions at the age of eight. In the center of the land is a flat-topped butte, and there are mountains in the distance, surrounding the viewer in all directions—an unusual geological feature that Rinpoche mentioned at the time. After he had lived in Arlee for a couple of years, he had—and has now achieved—a dream to build a statue garden of huge proportions on that piece of land. He called it the Magadha Garden of One Thousand Buddhas. The central statue, the Great Mother, standing over twenty-five feet tall, is filled with extremely holy relics, and is surrounded by the thousand buddhas of this aeon, as well as a thousand stupas.

Over the millennia, the Tibetans have developed to a high art the ability to fix and radiate pure realized mind. Through sacred

architecture, mantra (archetypal sound), and many other methods, they can ground that realized mind with a sort of giant tuning fork, which then sounds that note. Although we're not consciously aware of it, we have the ability to fall in tune with that note. Since everything emanates from pure mind/awareness, at our core we are pure mind as well. Because that true essence is covered over by distraction and confusion, we don't realize this true nature. Structures such as stupas and statues, filled with relics, "infect" us with the realization of that pure nature. We become entrained to that strong note being sounded, and naturally fall into a peaceful, happy, more awake state. We'll explore these ideas much further throughout this book. For now I'll just say that the relics are a key ingredient, as are the methods that expand the power of that ingredient.

A statue or stupa can be empowered in this way. Not only is Rinpoche aware of this phenomenon, but he has become a master at building stupas in order to help beings far into the future. After all, stupas last for hundreds, sometimes thousands, of years. With that ripple effect in mind, he has offered this pilgrimage site so that Americans can be "infected" by Buddha Mind, simply by bringing themselves there.

SCIENCE TIDBIT

Prayer Changing Water

I was fascinated to discover the work of Dr. Masaru Emoto. He spent many years photographing water before and after prayer had been directed at it or words had been pasted on the jars containing the water. He took microscopic photographs of the frozen water crystals before and afterward. The differences are dramatic.

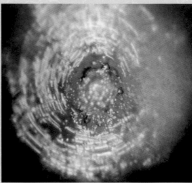

"*Thank You*"   "*You Fool*"

He tried the same sort of experiment with music, with similar effects.

Beethoven's Symphony No. 5   *Heavy Metal Music*

Some of you may also know of the work of Rupert Sheldrake, and the term he coined, *morphic resonance*, the title of his first book on the subject. His double-blind studies, which have been replicated world-wide, are accepted by many scientists.

In one experiment, he had people memorize lists of words, in a random order. The control group had a new list, and the experimental group had the list that other groups had been memorizing. The second group learned that same list faster, and subsequent groups even faster, as the experiment continued. The control groups learned at the same rate each time.

Other scientists who were working on crystal formation considered this a possible explanation for a phenomenon that had baffled them for decades. The first time they formed a new crystal pattern, it was extremely difficult to coax the substance to come together in that new formation. But as they formed that same one again and again, even in laboratories on different continents, with different scientists, it was progressively easier.

Sheldrake's theory was that these patterns are not localized—that *knowledge* is not localized. This would explain not only both of the above observations, but many other, previously unexplainable phenomena. For example, Sheldrake has since done many experiments with pets and their owners: though unable to see or hear each other, the pets somehow measurably respond to what is happening with their unseen owners. These results have been repeated again and again, with different pets and owners, in different locations.

Back to Dr. Emoto and his water crystals. His work became highly celebrated in Japan, and with his encouragement, thousands of people have conducted their own similar experiments. He even sold photographic equipment for the experiments on his website, producing more results supporting his theory that our thoughts and intentions have a measurable effect on water.

Given that it's water that he saw these results with, and water is the pervasive medium of life on Earth, the implications are huge. We ourselves are made up of more than two-thirds water, as is the food we eat.

One famous experiment was done with rice—this being Japan and all. Identical cooked rice was combined with the same kind of water and placed at the same time in two identical jars, one with "you fool" pasted on it, the other with "thank you." The rice was kept in the same room for one month. During this time several people talked to each jar, saying "You fool" to the "you fool" jar, and "Thank you" to the other. After one month, the "thank you" jar had turned a soft yellow and smelled sweetly fermented. The other had turned blackish and its smell was intolerable.

A far more dramatic experiment was done with one of the largest lakes in Japan, Lake Biwa. In July of 1999, 350 people gathered at the lake, which had become so polluted that the native plants had been overrun by an extremely foul-smelling algae called *kokanada*, nearly covering the lake. Every year the government would get calls from a large surrounding area, complaining of the fetid smell. No doubt the wildlife whose home was in and around the lake was also

"Thank You"   *"You Fool"*

affected. Though the government had spent large amounts of money in a heroic effort to discourage the algae, their efforts had had little effect. A widely known saying claimed that "if the water of Lake Biwa could be cleaned up, so could the rest of Japan's water." But no one knew how to make that happen. It seemed hopeless.

And so the crowd had gathered, armed with prayer and intention— nothing more, nothing less. After some instructions on breath control, they all repeated the Great Declaration ten times and cheered; then the prayer fest was over. The words to the Great Declaration, which helped the participants direct their thoughts and intentions, are "The eternal power of the universe has gathered itself to create a world with true and grand harmony."

Next summer, the *kokanada* was hardly to be found, and no one reported any foul smell. The government and scientists had no explanation. By August the phenomenon was being written up in the newspapers.

If the Buddha was right and we manifest our bodies from mind, and there really is one big awareness, then it all makes sense. If we see all this from only the view of Newtonian physics, which today's scientists no longer hold to be entirely true, then there is no explanation.

Though Dr. Sheldrake's work is accepted by many scientists, Dr. Emoto's is not as widely embraced. One sticking point is that Dr. Emoto didn't do double-blind studies: the people photographing the water knew which word was on which jar. According to the Heisenberg principle, the experimenter's own expectation and knowledge can affect the

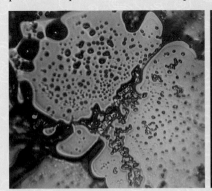 

Lake Biwa Water Before Prayer   *Lake Biwa Water After Prayer*

material being experimented on. But to my way of thinking, if that is indeed happening, wouldn't that further support Dr. Emoto's theory?

Another objection is that Dr. Emoto didn't let us see all of his photographs. Perhaps he picked out particular crystals to support his theory. That could be true. But now that home kits are available, and so many people are replicating his experiments and sharing their results, that concern has lessened in my mind. And if his theory were untrue, how could Lake Biwa have been transformed so dramatically and measurably? Still, I think it would be better if he had shared *all* of his photographs with scientists and others so that we could get a more complete understanding of the phenomenon.

That said, I do find the photographs and experiments he did show us compelling. The implications are powerful, not only for cleaning up water pollution. As one mother said regarding the sunflower that experimenters had attacked with the word *fool* for all its poor, stunted

As with many fathers, the king wanted to make sure the young prince went into the family business. As with many sons, Siddhartha had other leanings, but I'm getting ahead of myself.

To keep the young prince interested in worldly affairs, the king decided he needed to do two things. First, he needed to make sure Siddhartha never suffered, nor saw any suffering. Then he wouldn't feel moved by compassion to pursue a spiritual path. Second, he provided young Siddhartha with all the earthly pleasures one could possibly desire.

As the prince grew up, he never saw any old people, never saw anything die, and was surrounded by lavish beauty at every turn. By the time he was almost of marrying age, the king was throwing him huge parties, with multitudes of the most beautiful musicians and dancing girls.

Siddhartha was actually bored by all this. It was without meaning for him. He became restless, and began to pressure his father to let him go out and see the world. At first the king objected, but then he arranged a grand outing, taking great care to hide any suffering

whatsoever, and surrounding the prince with pleasurable things. They went on this grand outing, which was more like a parade than an exploration, and Siddhartha's restlessness only grew stronger. It was not to be denied.

An exceptional youth, stellar in intellectual, artistic, and athletic pursuits, Siddhartha knew perfectly well that everything around him was being orchestrated, contrived. He wanted to see the truth. He asked his charioteer to take him out of the palace secretly. The charioteer agreed.

Out they went, on the road to town. Before they'd gone very far, they came upon an old man, leaning on a stick. Siddhartha said, "Stop the chariot! What's wrong with that man?! His voice is hoarse, his hair is thin and white, his body is all twisted, and the little bit of flesh he has hangs from his bones in the strangest way. He can't walk without leaning on a stick. The poor man! What's happened to him?"

"That man is simply old," replied the charioteer. "He's lived maybe seventy or eighty years, and his body is falling apart. It happens to all of us, over time."

"No! Isn't there *something* we can do? Look how he's suffering with every step!"

"There's no cure for old age, or the pain and suffering that come from it. Our bodies fall apart after a while."

"Oh, this is awful. Every living being experiences this? I can't stand the thought of it! I've got to go home right now!"

The charioteer immediately took Siddhartha home, and he went straight to his room. He stayed there alone for days, overcome with grief for the pain of everyone and everything— any being who is born—suffering the deterioration of old age.

> "In the end what
> you don't surrender
> Well the world
> Just strips away."
>
> *Bruce Springsteen*

As you can imagine, the king was horrified. Since his son's birth, he'd lavished great expense and effort to keep all unpleasant sights from the palace grounds, yet his greatest fear was coming to pass. He ordered an even wider radius around the palace for banishment of all unpleasant sights.

confused dreamlike state that we mistake for true reality and that is actually the source of our suffering. He was now in a state of perpetual bliss, from which he never had to depart. He had now realized the secret of eternal happiness. He had attained it.

Shortly after his enlightenment, he was walking down the road. Struck by his brilliantly radiant presence and visible aura, a passerby stopped and asked him, "Are you a deity?"

"No."

"Are you a sorcerer, then?"

"No."

"An ordinary man?"

"No."

"Well, then, what are you?"

"I am awake."

In Sanskrit, the word for "awakened one" is *buddha*.

At that time he already had a few students. When they saw that he had gained total enlightenment and achieved eternal happiness, they said, "Please teach us, so we can be fully enlightened, too!"

"I would love to, if only I could portray it in words. True reality is beyond concepts. Anything we can think of, or put into words, is not true reality. In that case, how can I teach it, or even talk about it?"

"But you can't just *leave* us here to suffer and die, again and again! Please do *something* to help us!"

And so began the famous teachings of the Buddha, which we know today as the Dharma. In giving us the Dharma (literally, "truth" in Sanskrit), he gave us the methods by which we all can come to experience what he had experienced, the reality he now always abided in.

But he didn't ask them to practice these methods just because he said to; he felt that blind faith wasn't worth much. He asked them to try the methods for themselves, to see if they worked for *them*. The faith of our own experience is unshakable. We can't *unknow* something once we've come to know it for ourselves.

The Buddha lived, wrote, and taught these methods for many, many more years, establishing the first Buddhist Sangha, or spiritual community, the foundation for Buddhism as we know it today.

The three pillars common to all traditions within the Buddhist path are the Buddha, the Dharma, and the Sangha. Together they're called the Three Jewels. You've just now learned these words; later I'll explain why these three things are so very essential to our reaching the goal of this path. For now, let's go back to the Buddha.

Recognizing that we all have different styles of learning and different proclivities, he created a vast body of works, with several different basic courses of training, to meet our various needs. All of his many thousands of sutras and tantras have been saved and translated into all of the world's languages. All of the major methods for training the mind have been practiced, mastered, and carefully handed down, mouth-to-ear, mind-to-mind, from master to student, until the present day.

We can see, then, why the Buddha bothered to reach enlightenment. He had hoped from the outset of his quest that he could offer people a path other than running after happiness, only to bring more suffering on themselves in the process. He set out to help us to save ourselves from the painful cycle of birth, leading to old age, sickness, and death. Many have attained full enlightenment using his methods.

Even in recent times there have been eyewitness accounts of people attaining "rainbow body," leaving behind nothing but their hair and nails. Thousands of others showed signs of attaining enlightenment at the time of death, leaving mantra syllables on their bones and other physical marks.

So the Buddha Shakyamuni, as he is called by Tibetans, was spurred on by the highest motivation, known as the Two Purposes: enlightenment for self and enlightenment for others. He gained complete enlightenment in order to help all of the rest of us to be eternally happy and free of suffering, and to be more joyfully and compassionately alive as we make the journey toward enlightenment.

SUGGESTED READING

For a lovely introduction to the idea that happiness is something we can actually learn, just like playing the piano, I highly recommend the book *Happiness*, by Matthieu Ricard. It's short, to the point, and very readable, with lots of great stories and examples. Ricard also cites some fascinating recent studies on the effects of Buddhist practice on brain function. For example, wouldn't it be nice to be able to focus your mind on one thing and have it stay there? It's possible to train in that. But the trainings go far beyond that one capacity. His book tantalizes us with some of the results.

For example, chapter 16 quotes scientific studies on the brain that show off-the-charts positive brain functions in longtime meditators. Even fairly new meditators begin to show measurable results. If you're tempted to read chapter 16 first, it's all right with me. The books in this series give you some of the same beginning, traditional Tibetan mind-training methods that Ricard speaks of in his book and practices himself.

Ricard is a highly accomplished monk who trained and worked alongside Tulku Sangak Rinpoche, under His Holiness Dilgo Khyentse Rinpoche. Before he was a monk, he was a physicist. Tulku Sangak Rinpoche holds Ricard in the highest esteem.

Some of What the Buddha Saw
THE FOUR NOBLE TRUTHS

As you remember, when the Buddha first saw reality as it truly is, he was reluctant to try to put it all into words, a task he deemed impossible. Still, when his students begged him not just to leave them to wander hopelessly in Samsara, he began to teach.

From then until the end of his life, he taught the methods and understandings that, if his students held to them and followed them, could guide them to their own experience of true reality—enlightenment. Then no words would be necessary. They would not need to take anything on blind faith, because they would know for themselves, from their own experience.

As you've noticed, I've attempted to describe some key aspects of reality that the Buddha talked about, but of course the truth is much different from the words you've been reading. Not only is my explanation flawed because it's expressed in words, but more to the point, I'm only a sentient being lost in Samsara myself, not a buddha. Thankfully, as we all know, the Buddha did go on to teach the methods for seeing reality for ourselves, in all its truth and fullness. The first teaching he gave was the Four Noble Truths, which I'll just briefly introduce you to here. I strongly suggest you read about them in depth—for example, in *The Words of My Perfect Teacher* by Patrul Rinpoche or in the book and video *The Four Noble Truths* by His Holiness the Dalai Lama.

The Four Noble Truths are the *Truth of Suffering*, the *Truth of the Origin of Suffering*, the *Truth of the End of Suffering*, and the *Truth of the Path*.

STUDENT: *Is karma always negative?*

LT: There are both negative and positive traces we can put on our mindstream. The Tibetans generally use different words for each: *karma* for the negative, and *merit* for the positive. These work a lot like debit and credit, on a great karmic ledger. If there is a negative balance, we're either experiencing unhappy times, or we soon will be. When we finish a painful experience, that would indicate that we've paid that "karmic debt." On the other side, if we've been having a wonderful time and that comes to an end, we've just spent down some merit balance until it's exhausted. The workings of karma constitute a vast subject, and the Tibetans have looked into it quite deeply. I can only hope to introduce you and give you a general feeling for karma and merit in this book. I will say a bit more as we go along, though.

The Truth of the Origin of Suffering

This can be boiled down to the Three Poisons, which are the root causes of all the suffering of Samsara, the three categories of neurotic emotions: (1) ignorance/delusion, (2) desire/clinging, and (3) aversion/aggression. And these three, in turn, can be traced down to the Mother of All Root Causes: identifying as "I" instead of the whole ocean. One wave would be only one very small part of the vastness of the ocean. Yet our own "wave" fills our entire mental world—our movie is only about us. Actually, the real movie is about the entire ocean . . . which includes our own tiny wave. Quite a different viewpoint.

The secret is identifying with the whole ocean, instead of just one wave.

Remember, the word in Latin for "I" is *ego*. Maybe you've read or heard about "letting go of ego," or ego being the whole problem. It's not the ego, or anything else in existence, that's the problem. It's what we DO about it, first and foremost in our minds, that's the problem. It's the identifying as only being "I," and clinging to that "reality," that keeps us going around on the Wheel of Samsara.

The Truth of the End of Suffering

Here the Buddha was assuring us that we could indeed free ourselves from this Wheel of Samsara. Once the Buddha saw reality as it truly is and reached the point of no return (to Samsara), he was no longer tempted to follow after thoughts of grasping, aggression, and so on. He no longer had a reason to. The domino effect was reversed and stopped at its source.

We now know that, since we're made of Buddha Nature, we too can reach the end of all suffering, permanently. We can finally end our wandering and go back Home. For good.

The Truth of the Path

The Buddha laid out the actual methods for us to achieve this goal. He taught thousands and thousands of verses, including the sutras and tantras. In their various ways they outlined and explained the knowledge and methods that lead to enlightenment. The whole of his teachings is what is meant by the word *Dharma*, the "path" for the followers of the Buddha. As I said earlier, in Sanskrit, the word *Dharma* means "truth." In Tibetan it also means "phenomena." The homonym for the Tibetan word for Dharma—*chö*—means "to adjust" or "to correct." Anam Thubten Rinpoche points out that *chö* also means "to change, transform, from within." When we put all of these dimensions of meaning together, a richness emerges that in itself helps us on our way.

To give us more clarity about how to tread this path of liberation from Samsara, the Buddha laid out in his first teachings eight aspects, like eight strands woven together to make a very strong rope. He called them the Eightfold Noble Path: Right View, Right Thought, Right Speech, Right Conduct, Right Livelihood, Right Effort, Right Mindfulness, and Right Concentration. This is foundational to all branches of Buddhism, so there is a great deal written about this, but here I'm just mentioning it in the context of the Four Noble Truths.

If you'd like to explore this more, I highly recommend the piece "The Noble Eightfold Path" that a Western monk, Bhikkhu Bodhi, has written; he has written about the Eightfold Noble Path in a short online piece and as a more detailed book.

The Eightfold Noble Path is so foundational that I highly recommend that you read and contemplate it further. In general, again, these are all aspects of conduct that help us to tread the path of liberation from Samsara, from suffering, to perfect happiness that never ends. This, then, is the fourth Noble Truth—the Truth of the Path.

We can boil these Four Noble Truths down into one sentence: *once we understand the Truth of Suffering and the truth of its origins, we're ready to hear about the truth of the end of such sufferings and to tread the true path.*

Perhaps now it's clear why the Buddha started all his teachings with the Four Noble Truths.

The Two Truths

ABSOLUTE TRUTH & RELATIVE TRUTH

These Two Truths are not included in the Four Noble Truths; they are more like two different *realities* that the Buddha is referring to. Perhaps you've been wondering how to resolve the Absolute Truth that we've been talking about with your very real experience of actions and consequences, self and other, the more pedestrian everyday reality that somehow still seems awfully true. Good question! Actually, it's a huge question, one we won't fully succeed in resolving until we're fully certified buddhas.

What the Buddha had to say about this makes a lot of sense. He spoke of the *Two* Truths and warned that allegiance to only one will leave you in confusion. The first truth, known as Absolute (or Genuine

refined f
methods

Tibeta
and ther
deities a
some. F
evokes
ened n

As we
soun
dom
effe

I
as w
we
thi
th
of
e
o
a

or Ulti
thing e
Rel
ance—
about
ance:
fixat
thin
thin
we'
int
a r
ar
c

t

The Tibetans often do the practice of creating a colorful, elaborate, beautiful sand mandala. The artists work in such fine detail that some lines of color are as fine as one grain of sand. They sit for long hours, often with masks over their faces to muffle their breath so as not to disturb the sand, using tiny tubes to place the colored sand precisely. Such a sand mandala can take several artists several days or even weeks to create. Then at the end of the related ceremony, the entire mandala is thrown into a heap and tossed into a river.

I sat next to my father in the last month of his life, and was present just as he left his body. He didn't want to go. Of course I was going to miss him, but because of his long decline, I had already been missing him. What I felt most painfully was that I couldn't help him to let go. The day after I came home from the funeral I wrote this poem.

Even This Dream

Without food or drink for 10 days, now,
His entire occupation, winnowed down
    to breathing.
He puts his whole effort into this breath.
Then this one.
Staving off the inevitable, for
    one more breath.

The nurse comes in to take his vitals.
Yet another old man to check.
Saying, "He's comfortable."

This is *comfortable?*

He can't speak. She can't know,
Inside, the deep, far-reaching, kind hearted mind.

For minutes, hours,
Days, weeks,
I watch you by stages losing
The joy of chocolate
The joy of your wit
    making us laugh.

Long gone, the joy of travel
The joy of your work of
    helping others.

Tying your own shoes
Walking
Talking
Moving
Scratching where you itch.

It's all come down to breathing
With all your might.

Please, Dad, please
Let go.
Trade in this old body.

Let go into the loving infinite.
Home.
If only you knew,
That ending dreams
Means waking up.

If not, then starting another.

What keeps you here? Fear?
Of disappearing?
Of regrets weighing you?
Some combination of both.

This form that allows you
Entry into this dream,
Slowly, slowly, fallen apart.
A beautiful, beautiful dream.
You made it so.
I shared so much of it with you,
So gladly.

We don't want this dream to end.
But all dreams do.

Alas, alas,
Even this one too.

In the case of the mandala, we see that we're meant to enjoy and appreciate the exquisite beauty of this symbolic work of art. Yet we're not to cling.

This Poison very naturally leads to the remaining one: anger/ aversion (*shey-dang* in Tibetan), pushing away what we don't want, or pushing others out of the way of the things that we do want.

Here's an example of this toxic cycle at work:

Years ago, I was horrified when my darling, sweet little daughter wanted a block that a little boy was playing with. There was desire: she wanted the block. Of course he didn't want to relinquish it to her (his desire/clinging), so of course she yanked his hair. Not surprisingly, he screamed. It naturally followed from there that she got a time-out. So the whole drama began with (1) her "looking out for number one," (2) her grasping for the block so she could have it herself, and (3) her act of aggression, which led to (4) her own misery. This is the slippery slope in action: delusion, clinging, aggression, karmic action, resultant suffering. And besides, she never did get to play with that block.

We've all (for the most part) developed more subtle methods of grasping and repelling, but those driving emotions are still there, still leading to words and actions that over and over again cause dramas, and misery, for ourselves and others. We feel helplessly catapulted from one unhappy episode to another, unable to stop the cycle. The word for "Samsara" in Tibetan is *Korwa*, meaning "going around and around."

In case you were wondering, the Buddha was well aware that we don't have just three emotions. He spoke of 84,000 emotions, the full range, with fine degrees of subtlety. He grouped them into these three basic categories just so we could begin to get some clarity as to the workings of our own minds.

A Bit More about Karma

As in the example of my charming daughter (she's much more socially acceptable now, and has her own daughter to occasionally embarrass her), we know that thoughts, and the emotions that drive them, lead to action—karma. Just as in physics, for every action there's a reaction—or, as it's commonly expressed in the Dharma, for every action there's a result.

If the ocean of reality is really one great mind, then whatever one part of that mind says or does of course comes back to it. We *think* we're doing the action to somebody else, but that thought, word, or deed actually makes a trace on our own mindstream that we'll carry with us. We can't perceive those marks on our own mindstream; we experience them a little like when we smack a ball in a squash court and the ball eventually bounces its way back to us . . . usually from a different direction. We accept the physical laws of cause and effect, action and consequence. Yet we seem to find it baffling, and even unjust, when the same cause-effect principles apply predictably and inevitably to our actions toward other beings.

You see why they call them the Three Poisons. We poison ourselves with the misery of those feelings; then we commit actions that leave karmic traces on our own souls, leading to far more misery and keeping us going around and around. The other Tibetan name for these feelings that drive us is *nyön-mong.* In other English books on Tibetan Buddhism, you'll see that very important term translated as "afflictive emotions" (a term I often use) and "conflicting emotions," or even "neurotic emotions." Sometimes the word *passions* is used. The other term the Tibetans use, *Duk Sum,* translates directly as the Three Poisons.

From recent science, we know negative emotions can lead to health problems. From our own experience, we know how a bad feeling can poison our day, our interactions, and our relationships. From the point of view of karma, they poison us in an even deeper way. In this series I'll often use the term *Poisons.* In the next section you'll see more deeply why.

How We Stay Stuck

This law of cause and effect begins to explain why some people are born into comfortable circumstances and others into really awful ones . . . ONLY if I also put reincarnation into the picture. After all, how could a baby have caused a malformed leg or an abusive parent before they were born? Although we can all relate to the idea of causes being followed by results, the result doesn't always come immediately . . . or even within the same lifetime. That ball on a handball court could bounce a few times before arriving back at us. In our naïveté we think that once the ball leaves our hand, it goes away. But there isn't another handball court. There's only THE handball court.

To give you a quick definition of reincarnation, I'll stick with the metaphor of the waves on the ocean. When we watch a wave go up and then down, the actual water molecules in the wave when it comes up again are not the same. The wave isn't the same shape either. Yet there's *some* kind of momentum behind it that causes us to say that it's still the same wave. That thread of consciousness behind the various

lifetimes, the consciousness that leaves the body at death, and many of us say continues on, I call the *mindstream*. This is as clear and direct a translation of the Tibetan term as I can imagine.

I once asked my Root Lama, Tulku Sangak Rinpoche, how karma could follow us after death. If we, like a wave, sink back into the ocean of the emptiness/awareness after this life, how can we reemerge into the next life with the karma from this life? He gave me a visual. He picked up a piece of paper and rolled it into a tube. Then he laid it flat again. The ends curled up. He then flattened it for a moment. It popped back up. To that demonstrative metaphor I've added the idea of a crease. Again, after flattening the paper, we still see the crease of each act, along with any curls of habit.

That little demonstration showed me how our thoughts, words, and deeds create traces on our own mindstreams, and our habits of mind shape them, so that even after our respite in the ocean of one awareness, we reemerge with a similar shape of mind, with karmic traces (creases) still there. Each of us usually has a favorite among the Three Poisons that shapes both the mind and body we create.

In almost every case, those shapes and creases don't disappear until we live out the results of the actions that formed them. The Bible says, "Ye shall reap what ye sow." On the other side of the world, the Tibetans also use the metaphor of planting seeds and harvesting fruits. We don't get an apple when we plant a thistle. In our mistaken efforts to be self-serving, we plant thistles all the time, expecting apples. We resent that we end up with thistles.

When I first spent some time with Rinpoche, I heard many stories of the horrors of his life after the occupation of Tibet. He was in prison for nearly ten years, couldn't contact his family, lived under horrible conditions, did hard labor, and was tortured, scorned, and beaten. As a psychotherapist, I naturally looked for signs of post-traumatic stress disorder (PTSD). Try as I might, I couldn't see any. Much later, Rinpoche told me that most Tibetans didn't have PTSD after such traumatic experiences. At one point, a group of psychotherapists volunteered to come to Dharamsala to greet Tibetans as they fled the turmoil in their country and escaped over the Himalayas. They expected to do some trauma work, but they, too, found almost no signs—despite horrors often worse than what Rinpoche experienced.

His Holiness the Dalai Lama and his people theorized that because the concepts of reincarnation and karma are so much a part of Tibetans, they simply saw the suffering as the ripening of some actions they'd committed in another life, since "beginningless time." This allowed them to make some sense of things, retain their self-esteem as *this* person in *this life*, and also to feel compassion for their captors, who, after all, were sowing seeds for horrible suffering for themselves in the future. Besides, the Tibetans couldn't say they were any better, since they'd obviously done something like that in another life, themselves.

This wasn't just pleasant Sunday school theorizing; this was a powerful worldview that met the painful daily reality they were living. They mostly emerged from terrible suffering as intact, compassionate people. I think of the contrast between that and some Jews who speak of not forgiving God for the Holocaust (as though some Heavenly Father ordered it) and various Judeo-Christians who have PTSD decades after a trauma, get cancer, lose a loved one, and smolder with resentment, saying, "Why me?"

No matter where we are, or in what circumstances, we all have our ways of misguidedly pursuing happiness, all the while sowing seeds of misery. The key is that, since we identify with this tiny apparition we call "me," we pursue happiness for *ourselves*.

Have you ever noticed that the people who help others seem to be the happiest? People serving mainly their own desires don't seem to be as happy, no matter how furiously they pursue their own ends. We can only speculate, but the Dalai Lama sure *seems* to be happy all the time. Everyone gets infected by his joyful presence. This despite the fact that he has lost his country, and the Tibetan religion and culture are dying out before his eyes. On the other hand, when Hitler was at his height, he was famous for his fits of temper. I doubt he was actually very happy.

One Tibetan monk said that once he could see the suffering on the face of his torturer, he was able to have compassion for him.

If we saw ourselves as the whole ocean, we'd already be happy and wouldn't need to be so busy pursuing anything. And of course, we'd think only in terms of happiness *for all*. In that case, why would we ever do something that would harm another? Would we even think in terms of "other"? When would we ever act without the motivation to benefit all?

So this is essentially how we stay stuck in Samsara, or the Wheel of Samsara: because as we chase after happiness, we keep sowing seeds of misery. Through ignorance/delusion (one of the Three Poisons), we see things through our twisted karmic lens. Then, in this deluded state, we're driven by desire (another Poison), as well as anger/aversion (the remaining one). We follow our thoughts to their confused conclusions, then act in misguided ways that sow more karmic

This is how
we stay stuck
in Samsara

seeds. Then we reap those, try to relieve the misery in the wrong way, do all that habitually, and around and around we go.

The Buddha had been on that wheel, but finally saw through the dream—gave it up altogether—and reached the point of no return, freeing him to rest in an indescribably joyful state permanently. Lucky for us—incalculably lucky—he didn't just let go and turn into rainbow light as he melted into the great ocean of oneness. Most who have attained enlightenment do that. But the Buddha carried into his last life the powerful momentum of lifetimes of compassionate intent. Even after reaching full Buddhahood, he stayed in that body and taught us the way out.

STUDENT: *If we'd be so much happier giving up identifying with ego, and we're so miserable with it, why don't we all just give it up? What's the big deal?*

LT: The short answer: Go for it! The long answer: When great masters have become enlightened, they've reported that it was a very simple moment, like letting a heavy coat drop off of you when it gets warm. The problem for the rest of us is that we're so entrenched in the reality of being this one little apparition—since beginningless time—that the idea of dropping it feels like obliteration. Since we can't really feel the whole ocean of compassionate awareness, it seems to us like we'll *vanish altogether*, and be no more. This is why we cling so desperately to our small, separate self, even in times of extreme misery. No matter how many times we read or hear that we're better off identifying with the whole ocean, and believe it with our conscious, rational mind, too much of our mindstream—our habitual, small mind—still clings to the self-perpetuating conviction that we're a separate, distinct self.

There is a Sanskrit term that puts its finger right on this conviction: *satkaya-drsti*. "*Sat* means real or true, *kaya*, body, and *drsti* is view; the term as a whole is usually translated 'personality-belief.'"*

When my daughter was fifteen years old, she took refuge with Rinpoche in a ceremony in Nepal. That night, as we were falling asleep, she said, "Mama, I really feel as if it wouldn't be a big deal to just drop it all—all that I think is me—and join with everything. But as soon as I actually try to *do* it, I realize I'm too scared." She was a very wise fifteen-year-old.

---

*   *Sangharakshita, What Is the Sangha?*

eye we look and act like an ordinary stone. We need to smelt the ore, to get rid of the nonessential elements and end up with the pure gold. In our case, we need to apply skillful methods so we can eventually, ultimately, refine the gold of our true selves. So enlightenment generally doesn't happen in an instant of epiphany. It's a process, just like discovering, smelting, and refining gold.

Interestingly, there were time-honored schools of alchemy in both the West and the East. Carl Jung revived those studies in the West, realizing that the "gold" the alchemists had been really concerned with was not metal; it was the soul, restored to its original purity. These alchemists' goal was very much like the refining to perfection of the mindstream that we've been talking about.

To put it simply, we need to remove the impurities of ego identification, to allow the pure gold of our true nature to shine forth, unimpeded.

The process of changing age-old habits of mind can't be instantaneous, though the last moment of crossing over to enlightenment is. Sure, it takes time and effort. But again, the question I asked myself when I set out on this journey was, "Do I have something *better* to do?"

Another traditional analogy I like is that of the sun and clouds. When clouds obscure the sun, it looks as if the sun has disappeared. But we know it's still there, shining just the same. It's just that our vision is obscured by the clouds. And even on a cloudy day, it isn't pitch dark—we can still find our way if we watch where we're going.

So it is with us. Even as we are right now, we have buddha qualities, evidence that we're really made of Buddha Nature. Whenever we go out of our way during the day to help someone—and feel a warm, happy feeling when we do—we know we're not really so separate after all. When a stray puppy is hungry and lonely, our hearts are moved by compassion. When we feel moved by the suffering and death of people hit by a tsunami in Japan, and we've never met them and don't speak their language, why is that? According to Buddhism, it's because deep in our truest essential self, we're not actually separate from them. Many waves, one ocean.

> Our true nature is Buddha Nature.

And you're taking the time and effort to read this book because some essential core in you knows the truth and is seeking it. When something rings true, what part of ourselves recognizes it?

I see all of these as hints that, despite the endless lifetimes in confusion, our true nature is Buddha Nature.

As we've learned, *buddha* means "awakened one." The Tibetan word for buddha is *sang-gye*, which can be broken into two parts: *sang*, meaning "cleansed," and *gye*, which means "fully matured"—in other words, *cleansing* away the clouds of karmically tainted perception and *fully maturing* our buddha (awakened) qualities.

The Three Kayas

Once the Buddha was able to see with absolutely no veils, he saw that reality is one vast ocean of awareness. It actually has no solid substance, yet isn't just a blank vacuum.

It's aware.

Its natural quality is endless compassion, for there is truly no separation: what is felt by one part of reality is felt by the whole vast awareness.

By its nature and power, it constantly manifests appearances, just as the ocean constantly manifests waves. As we're learning more and more in subatomic physics, we're seeing (as the Buddha saw 2,500 years ago) that these appearances aren't the substantial things we thought they were at all.

The celebrated science writer Loren Eiseley tells this story:

> In the more obscure scientific circles which I frequent there is a legend circulating about a late distinguished scientist who, in his declining years, persisted in wearing enormous padded boots much too large for him. He had developed, it seems, what to his fellows was a wholly irrational fear of falling through the interstices of that largely empty molecular space which common men in their folly speak of as the world. A stroll across his living-room floor had become, for him, something as dizzily horrendous as the activities of a window washer on the Empire State Building. Indeed, with equal reason he could have passed a ghostly hand through his own ribs.

David Bohm found confirmation of his mystic vision on television in the 1960s, when he saw a device made of two concentric glass cylinders, the space between them filled with colorless glycerin. The experimenter put a drop of ink in the glycerin, and then turned the outer cylinder. As a result, the droplet was drawn out into a thread, which gradually became thinner and thinner until it vanished completely; the ink had disappeared but still existed in the glycerin. When the cylinder was turned in the opposite direction, the ink reappeared from its enfolded, hidden existence. Bohm realized that there was no disorder or chaos, but, rather, a hidden order.

To us it would've just been a kind of cool thing. To Dr. Bohm it was life-changing. Bohm writes that "when the ink drop was spread out, it still had a 'hidden' (i.e., non-manifest) order that was revealed when it was reconstituted." After trying for years to explain many things that had remained steadfastly beyond his understanding, he now had a clue for an explanation. Then he got an even better clue: holograms.

Shortly after holographic photography was invented, I went to a laboratory where scientists were experimenting with it. They enthusiastically showed me a piece of holographic film with an image on it. It looked pretty much like any other flat piece of film, and all I could see were lots of concentric circles of various sizes, as in a pond just after a few pebbles are thrown in. I tried to look impressed. Then they shined a laser beam through it. Appearing in thin air in front of the film was a 3-D picture of chess pieces on a chess board. I was more impressed.

Then they showed me how, even if you cut that film in half, the *whole image* still shows through either half. You just have to lean a little to the left or right to see the whole thing, as though you were looking through a window that was smaller than the scene. Sure enough: I leaned side to side, seeing more of the image that had been hidden. Now I was every bit as excited as the scientists!

How does this work? Well, it's a long story, but I'll try to give you an idea in this small space. The pond circles I'd first seen, as they fanned out, crossed each other. These created incalculably complicated "interference patterns," as they're called. In those patterns was far more information than on normal photographic film. These holograms stored the exponentially greater information needed to depict three dimensions, unfolded into the actual image only when the laser beam shone through it. Even more fascinating is that *every bit of the film contained the whole.* Hence the name.

That's why the half piece of film I'd looked through contained the whole picture. Perhaps you can see why Bohm got excited about holograms. Here I can't help but quote Talbot directly:

> One of Bohm's most startling assertions is that the tangible reality of our everyday lives is really a kind of illusion, like a holographic image. Underlying it is a deeper order of existence, a vast and more primary level of reality that gives birth to all the objects and appearances of our physical world in much the same way that a piece of holographic film gives birth to a hologram. Bohm calls this deeper level of reality the *implicate* (which means "enfolded") order, and he refers to our own level of existence as the *explicate*, or unfolded, order.

This theory helps explain many phenomena previously unexplained by science. Though I won't go on about them all here, you can explore them through Talbot's work, and, of course, Bohm's.

I do want to quote Talbot's explanation of one previously unexplained phenomenon, because it more thoroughly clarifies the confounding conundrum of waves vs. particles—sometimes whimsically called "wavicles."

> It also explains how a quantum can manifest as either a particle or a wave. According to Bohm, both aspects are always enfolded in a quantum's ensemble, but the way an observer interacts with the ensemble determines which aspect unfolds and which remains hidden. As such, the role an observer plays in determining the form a quantum takes may be no more mysterious than the way a jeweler who manipulates a gem determines which of its facets become visible and which do not.

Perhaps this is how we can use scientific theory to illuminate the interaction between the ocean and its waves that Buddhism speaks of. Perhaps this helps us understand, too, how we create and project our own reality from the infinite possibilities enfolded within the one great awareness.

Bohm saw that the universe is constantly weaving between the implicate and explicate. For this ever-changing, moving phenomenon that Bohm wanted to point to, he wasn't satisfied with the limited, static term *hologram*. He invented the term *holomovement*.

The Tibetans speak of three basic facets of reality—the Three Kayas. The emptiness/awareness facet is called the *Dharmakaya*, or Truth Body. It's the ultimate, true basis behind the appearances we see.

The "waves," or appearance, aspect is divided into two more facets. One is the *Sambhogakaya*, or Body of Complete Abundance; the other is the *Nirmanakaya*, or Emanation Body. As we turn our attention from emptiness into form, we come first to Sambhogakaya. Perhaps this one is like Bohm's implicate order (see "A Modern Physics Take—Holomovement"). The translator Sangye Khandro has sometimes described it as the Illusory, Blissful Being. How evocative! It's sort of like a template through which the power of that vast awareness can emanate into form. We don't have this exact concept in the West, but we do have a relatively new term that comes close.

You may have heard of the Western term *archetype*, popularized by Carl Jung, speaking of essential principles, such as the Great Mother principle, or the King, the Maiden, the Wise Man, and so on. We can't experience the archetypal level directly because we're stuck on the Nirmanakaya level of more fully manifested appearances—perhaps like Bohm's explicate order—as seen through our spattered windshields. Oh, if only we had a "channel changer" for the Kayas! This would be so much easier.

Given that we don't have a Kaya channel changer—*yet*, anyway—we can get only a subtle experience of an *archetype itself*, through an archetypal image. That's why we feel inspired when we look at some image of the Great Mother: for example, the Chinese image of Quan Yin or an image of the Virgin Mary tends to evoke the felt experience of the purer Great Mother archetype. Though we don't have the channel changer, we use archetypal image, sound, and myth to "tune in" to the archetype itself. With very skillful methods and lots of practice, we can eventually learn to change channels at will.

But for most of us, it isn't just that we've lost the channel changer. To make matters worse, our vision is extremely altered, like a really warped, dirty, spattered, tinted windshield. What we see—though it seems absolutely real to us—has little resemblance to the Three Kayas seen with pure vision, as they truly are. Perhaps this problem relates to Bohm's theory that there are different facets of an "ensemble" contained within the implicate, and that an observer can tune in to one or another facet. So why do we zero in on one facet and not another?

Carl Jung. (Demitri Kessel/The Life Picture Collection/Getty Images)

Presumably, it has something to do with the shape of our own mind. Habitual points of view, for example. Our habits of *how* we chase after happiness and run from suffering determine what channel we'll fixate on. For many lifetimes we've had a vested interest in how things are going on around us—is it good for me or bad for me? This causes the fixation, making it impossible for us to freely change channels. Note that, since we don't have the channel changer, we're not *deciding* which channel, or facet, to tune in to; we fall into a channel and tend to stay stuck there, believing that's just reality . . . until we die and are forced to leave that particular show.

If we start with the Dharmakaya level, the emptiness/awareness level, we then go through the archetypal-template level (Sambhogakaya), and then on to the more complex and fully manifest Nirmanakaya level. Remember that, just as the ocean and its waves aren't really separate, the Kayas are also just different aspects of the same thing—like the sun and its rays, or two sides (and the rim?) of one coin. The Kayas themselves—the ocean and its waves—are all perfectly pure; we just can't see them that way. Once we clean our windshield, we'll find the channel changer again and see the Kayas in all their vast, pristine, and beautiful perfection. That's what the Buddha did.

The Five Timeless Awarenesses (Yeshes)

How does this really work? Well, since we can't experience it all very directly, it's no wonder the Buddha couldn't fully put this reality into words that would make us *see* it. Words themselves carry concepts warped and colored by our delusion (and different delusions and colorations for each of us), so there's a catch-22. Nevertheless, we can continue to use metaphor to point us in the right direction.

Another aspect of the vast Dharmakaya is a quality of wisdom/awareness that the Tibetans call *yeshe*, or "primordial wisdom." *Yeshe* has sometimes been translated as "wisdom" or "timeless awareness" (my personal favorite).

This yeshe first divides into primal, archetypal principles of reality, spoken of as the "Five Yeshes." These can appear as lights of five different colors, and many people have reported seeing them in near-death experiences, as well as in visions. Interestingly, people of various cultures and religions have spoken of them in pretty much the same way.

The play of yeshe continues. These Five Yeshes weave together into an increasingly complex and dense tapestry until we get to the level of fully emanated Nirmanakaya, the waves part of the ocean. Compassion pervades the entire vast ocean of play.

The moment we move our focus from the unity of the Dharmakaya to the Five Yeshes, we're no longer in the formless, unified Dharmakaya territory; we're speaking of the Sambhogakaya.

Here the yeshe of the Dharmakaya now is like a five-faceted jewel: the Yeshe of Basic Space, Mirrorlike Yeshe, the Yeshe of Equality, Discerning Yeshe, and All-Accomplishing Yeshe.

Now that we're in the area of archetype (Sambhogakaya), the one state of Buddhahood is divided into the same five facets, the Five Dhyani Buddhas that are lords of the Five Buddha Families. Their names are Vairochana, Amitabha, Akshobhya, Ratnasambhava, and Amogasiddhi.

These buddhas each have their own respective purelands, and their consciousness pervades the universe. They and their respective yeshes are principles of reality—like fundamental archetypes—which Tibetan Buddhism makes easier to work with by applying archetypal images. They're each associated with qualities of being, colors, directions, and countless other things. They weave together in ever more complex forms to create all that appears.

Because they're not separate from anything, they feel the suffering of all the lost beings just as if it were their own . . . for it is. Out of this ultimate kind of compassion that is ceaseless and endless, they are constantly weaving together all appearances—the waves of the ocean. To my mind, this idea of the Three Kayas goes beyond Bohm's concept of implicate and explicate order. Bohm points the way for Western minds, but the understanding of the Three Kayas is more fully developed, and *alive*.

Of course, because of our warped and spattered lenses, we can't see all this as it really is. We only see our own deluded dream. Not only do things appear in a very warped way, but we can only see things on the channel that we're fixated on . . . and we've lost the channel changer! Perhaps Bohm would say that, out of the complex array of possible facets of an "ensemble" that can "unfold" into matter, the observer's own habits of mind determine which facets will appear to their eye.

How could there be any hope of finding our way out of this dream?

As I said, the archetypal, or Sambhogakaya, level is generally impossible for us to perceive directly, but it is still very powerful and compelling, still very much at work, like a prevailing current beneath the waves of the ocean, affecting the formation of the waves on a vast scale.

From our confused, fixated vantage point of the Nirmanakaya level, we can work through archetypal images, as with the earlier examples of the Great Mother archetype, so we can actually perceive something helpful from within our own dream.

In all the world's great religions, we find archetypal images of the Great Mother, such as the Virgin Mary, Quan Yin, and, in Tibetan Buddhism, Green Tara or Yum Chenmo. Our first archetypal *image* of the Great Mother is most often the face of our own mother; we already have a space in the deep recesses of our minds for the Great Mother archetype, and the image—our mother's face, and, later, cultural and artistic expressions—fills that space. Through an image we've made this connection with, we feel the vast power of the archetype itself.

Then we have our various dramas around that archetype, through the image. Archetypes are a stronger driving force behind our lives than we're conscious of, like an ocean current pulling and driving the waves along. Rather than be driven by archetypes in an unconscious, usually harmful way, why not use them to help us toward enlightenment? Why not use them to live more skillfully right now?

We imagine all kinds of things and live out experiences in our minds countless times, every day of our lives . . . and at night in our dreams. Wouldn't it be nice if we could *choose* which experiences to have? The Buddha, as well as the Tibetan masters, was fully aware of this phenomenon, and created practices that take full advantage of it.

The Five Dhyani Buddhas

As I've said, once yeshe has divided into its five aspects, those five basic principles of reality, those Five Yeshes, have distinct qualities of awareness. To give us a way of relating to them on this level, we speak of the Five Dhyani Buddhas. We picture yeshe (timeless awareness, or wisdom) which of course is enlightened mind, as a buddha sitting there, with particular clothes, mantra sounds, and other characteristics that evoke the actual archetype. Each of the buddhas is the color of one of the five lights, and each can be found in their own Buddhafield, or pureland. The Five Yeshes are referred to as "families." I've listed them for you in the adjacent chart, though once again, words are of course inadequate.

The Five Buddha Families*

Family	*Head of Family* (Male, Female)	*Yeshe Quality*	*Afflictive Emotion*
Buddha	Nampar Nang-Dzey, Namka Ying-Chukma	Yeshe of Basic Space	Delusion, Laziness, Stupidity
Lotus	Nangwa Tayey, Gö Karmo	Discerning Yeshe	Desire, Longing, Clinging
Vajra	Mi-Kyödpa, Sangye Chenma	Mirrorlike Yeshe	Anger, Aversion
Jewel	Rinchen Jungden, Mamaki	Equalizing Yeshe	Pride, Inflation
Karma	Dönyöd Drupa, Damtsik Drölma	All-Accomplishing Yeshe	Competitiveness, Jealousy

See Sanskrit equivalents in glossary.

I think of these as five basic qualities, or flavors, of enlightened mind. They weave themselves into more and more complex forms. The chart indicates how they appear to us (in our confusion) as the five elements (the four we know of, plus space), the seasons, the bodily humors, the four directions plus center for the fifth, etc., etc. In fact, these five principles of reality weave themselves together into all the forms of the Nirmanakaya . . . including our own physical bodies. Hence the name *Nirmanakaya*, or Emanation Body. Again, I see a correlation between Emanation Body and Bohm's explicate. But there is a vast difference between the dense bodies we think we and others have, and the non-solid, light bodies that we'd see without our spattered windshields in the way.

In sitting with this chart, maybe you can determine which family is your primary one. Tibetan medical doctors believe their patients to have manifested their bodies from their minds. If that's the case, then the habits and tendencies of our minds are also going to manifest in our bodies.

For example, a person more strongly aligned with the Vajra family will tend to have anger as their prominent emotion. This is because,

Color	Direction	Element	Symbol
Blue	Center	Space	Wheel
Red	West	Fire	Lotus
White	East	Water	Vajra
Yellow	South	Earth	Jewel
Green	North	Air	Crossed Vajras

concentrated and powerful medicine, there's less risk of damage (harder to OD on cough drops than on beta-blockers). It's easy to think, "Oh, I've distilled my anger to Mirrorlike Yeshe on this one," when in fact you just haven't. The lama would probably see that and point it out to you, and you would have to take a more honest, though less comfortable, look.

It's a bit like the sorcerer's apprentice, playing with something very powerful but not fully knowing how to wield that power. Another example is the story of Icarus, who didn't listen to his father's advice and flew too close to the sun, melting his wings and falling into the sea.

One feature that helps us stabilize ourselves on the Vajrayana path is that, as I've mentioned, it actually contains the other two within it. Especially in the earlier stages, we do many of the same practices that are done in Theravada, though in slightly different styles.

I don't know about you, but I would feel a lot better following the Vajrayana path if there were a way to keep me from going off track. Fortunately there is a very effective one: the lama. A lama performs several functions similar to those of a typical minister, but also serves as a teacher and guide for students on the particular path to Vajrayana Buddhism.

Lama Tsomo translating for Rinpoche at the ground consecration for the Namchak Retreat Ranch

Of course, you have to make sure you've found a qualified lama. You would want the lama to be well trained in the practices, have actually accomplished the practices, know the theoretical foundation, have sufficiently worked on themselves that their own Buddha Nature is evident, and be proceeding from motives that are pure.

If a lama has all of the above qualifications, is of a lineage you are drawn to, and you feel some connection, then they can be immensely helpful as your spiritual friend and guide.

Since they've worked deeply and intensely with their own Three Poisons and have successfully used proven methods to distill them, they can see when you might be off track and how you might right yourself. There is no substitute for your regular connection with a live lama. Not all of the teachings are written down, for the very purpose of making sure the student learns from a qualified lama and doesn't proceed into powerful and risky territory unguided. Because of this intention, even the scriptures that teach practices always leave the most important parts out.

But beyond being a safety net, the lama provides us with a projection screen for *our own Buddha Nature*, which we can't see very well. If we could see it perfectly well, we wouldn't still be here in Samsara.

Yet another benefit we gain from our lama is that, if we truly join our minds with them, we can piggyback onto their level of realization. No kidding. I learned this one by sort of stumbling upon it.

I had been studying with Rinpoche for a few months, doing Guru Yoga, which is the practice of joining one's mind with the lama, in my daily meditation sessions. The next part of my session was the actual meditation. An odd thing was happening during the meditation part. My awareness was far beyond anything I'd experienced before and somehow didn't feel like my own mind that I was so familiar with. It was striking and lovely—very freeing. I called Rinpoche to ask him what that was.

"You've been doing Guru Yoga, right?"

"Yes."

"And you've been connecting with my mind during Guru Yoga?"

"Yes."

"Well, then you're feeling a connection with my level of realization," he said, in a very matter-of-fact way. To him as a Tibetan lama, this was everyday meat and potatoes. To me it was mind-blowing.

Now perhaps you've gotten a taste of the Three Yanas, and where Vajrayana falls within that.

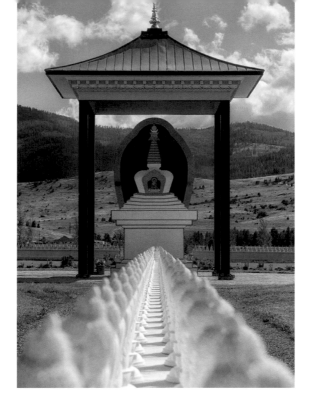

CONCLUSION

So this is a bit of what the Buddha saw. Luckily for us he didn't leave us hanging, but gave us the methods so we can see it for ourselves and reach enlightenment ourselves. If you find that some of what you've encountered here rings true for you, and you'd like to road test a method or two, we at the Namchak Foundation have done some work to support you in that! And of course, you can peruse the very large buffet from various Buddhist and meditation groups. Ours can be found at our website, Namchak.org, where we have eCourses, a newsletter, and people to facilitate your finding a small study group to compare notes with. You can also begin Book 2 in this series, which launches right into three foundational practices to try for yourself!

Whatever your next step, I hope you found inspiration and food for thought in this book. Wherever you go from here, I wish you a meaningful and satisfying journey, that's just right for *you*.

Appendix A: Glossary

Absolute Truth (Tibetan: *dön-dam-denba*): The abiding truth, not subject to a particular deluded being's point of view. The reality perceived by enlightened beings. *See also* Two Truths.

Archetype: Jungian term describing a sort of lens that acts as a template, shaping generalized consciousness into a more particular principle of reality with particular characteristics—for example, the Great Mother archetype or the Wise Man archetype—which one can find in images and stories throughout human societies.

Bodhicitta [bo-di-CHIT-ta] (Sanskrit; "Mind of Enlightenment/Awakening"): "On the relative level, it is the wish to attain Buddhahood for the sake of all beings, as well as the practice of the path of love, compassion, the six transcendent perfections, etc., necessary for achieving that goal. On the absolute level, it is the direct insight into the ultimate nature." (from *The Words of My Perfect Teacher* by Patrul Rinpoche, trans., Padmakara Translation Group.) It is the motivation to help others. It naturally flows from our own Buddha Nature, which *feels* how we're not separate from others.

Buddha (Sanskrit; "Awakened One"): A being who has reached full enlightenment by cleansing all adventitious *lo-bur* ("baggage"), such as karma and bad habits of the mind, and has fully brought forth—matured—their Buddha Nature. It is predicted that there will be over a thousand who will reach this state in this *kalpa*, or aeon. Note: The buddha who created the religion and methods of Buddhism and taught the sutras and tantras was the Buddha Shakyamuni.

Buddha Nature (Tibetan: *deshek nyingpo*): Our essential nature, which is not separate from the Dharmakaya and is the seed of our own complete enlightenment.

Dharma (Sanskrit): A general term for the teachings and path of the Buddha Shakyamuni.

Dharmakaya (Sanskrit; literally "Truth Body"): The vast, pregnant emptiness out of which everything arises. It is not a dead vacuum, but pure, essential awareness. It is beyond defining but has many qualities. It is vast without limit; ultimate compassion, ultimate unity, pure potential, all-knowing, the ultimate root of all. At this level there is no form; there is unity. It is no different from complete Buddhahood.

Five Dhyani Buddha Families: For each of these five categories, or families, there is a particular buddha, color, direction, and many other characteristics. These are the Sanskrit Buddha Family names (male, female). The Tibetan names appear in the chart on pages 106–107.

1. Buddha: Vairochana, Dhatishvari
2. Lotus: Amitabha, Pandaravasini
3. Vajra: Akshobhya, Buddhalochana
4. Jewel: Ratnasambhava, Mamaki
5. Karma: Amogasiddhi, Samayatara

The Five Buddha Families weave together, along with all their qualities and characteristics, to create the complex appearances of manifested reality.

Karma (Sanskrit; "action"): In this context it refers not only to actions but to their natural consequential effects. Think "Ye shall reap what ye sow."

Lama (Tibetan): A title equivalent to *rabbi* or *minister*. In Vajrayana the lama is often more of a spiritual mentor than their Christian counterpart or than in Theravada Buddhism.

Mahayana (Sanskrit; "Great Vehicle"): That branch of Buddhism which has the Two Purposes as motivating factors: enlightenment for self *and* for others. In every school of Mahayana Buddhism, one takes a vow to help *all* beings toward enlightenment.

Merit: Positive effects of actions, in particular. Like an entry appearing in the credit column of the karmic "ledger."

Mindstream: That bit of awareness that inhabits the body but isn't actually *of* the body, and that experiences lifetime after lifetime.

Ngöndro [NGÖN-dro] (Tibetan; "Preliminary Practices"): These are practiced after Shiney and before more advanced practices. Actually, Ngöndro is incorporated into the beginning of advanced practices too—hence the name.

Nirmanakaya (Sanskrit; "Emanation Body"): The manifestation level/aspect of shining forth from the Dharmakaya/Buddhahood. Another, further order of complexity of form, as compared with the Sambhogakaya. Perceptible to sentient beings in a warped and confused way, depending on their own karmically and habitually distorted "lens."

Original Purity (Tibetan: *kadak*): An intrinsic quality of the Dharmakaya and all that issues from it. This, of course, includes human beings.

Relative Truth (Tibetan: *kün dzop denba*): The reality perceived by sentient beings in their deluded state. *See also* Two Truths.

Rinpoche [RIN-po-chey]: An honorific term used for high lamas—higher than the Christian term *reverend*, but lower than *His Holiness*. Most lamas are not referred to by this title, only the most accomplished.

Root Lama: Root guru. An individual spiritual guide and mentor. This is arguably the most intimate and karmically significant of human relationships.

Sambhogakaya (Sanskrit; literally "Body of Complete Enjoyment"): The first level/aspect of spontaneous shining forth into form, from the Dharmakaya. Similar to the archetypal level of being that Jungians speak of. Rarely directly perceptible to human beings.

Samsara (Sanskrit): The cycle of existence—of birth, death, and rebirth—in which all sentient beings find ourselves. We are propelled from one situation to the next by our own deluded thoughts, negative emotions, karma, and habits of mind, from which we perform actions that, in turn, create further karmic consequences. We then react to these, mentally, emotionally, and physically. These in turn create ceaseless experiences in existence, like a self-perpetuating dream, until we finally wake up (and, as His Holiness the Dalai Lama says, "Better it be sooner").

Sangha (Sanskrit): The spiritual community.

Shamata (Sanskrit; (Tibetan: *Shiney*); "Tranquil Abiding Meditation") A meditation that is practiced, in similar forms, in all branches of Buddhism. It is taught to new practitioners in Vajrayana. Its endeavor is to calm the flow of thoughts while heightening mindfulness. Eventually, through this training, one can focus attention on one thing and have it stay there, in a clear, unperturbed, joyfully peaceful state.

Sutra [SOO-tra]: The original teachings of the Buddha.

Tantra [TAHN-tra]: Further teachings of the Buddha, which are not studied or practiced by the Theravadins but are the mainstay of Vajrayana—Tibetan Buddhism.

Theravada [teh-ra-VA-da] (Sanskrit; "Root, or Foundational Vehicle, School of the Elders"): The foundational-level branch of Buddhism, common to all branches. Of the three main branches of teachings of the Buddha Shakyamuni, it was the first to be taught. It is based on the sutras and does not include the tantras; the motivation for enlightenment is focused on one's own liberation from Samsara.

Three Jewels: The Buddha, the Dharma, and the Sangha—in which all Buddhists have vowed to take refuge until reaching complete enlightenment. The thought is that the combination of all three will greatly help us along the way: the Buddha because he has achieved enlightenment himself, so has proven to know the way; the Dharma because it is the instructions, or "map," that he provided us; and the Sangha, or spiritual community, as companions along the way.

Three Kayas: *See* Dharmakaya, Samboghakaya, Nirmanakaya.

Three Poisons, a.k.a. *afflictive emotions* (Tibetan: *nyön-mong*): The Buddha (Shakyamuni) grouped the thousands of emotions, like fear, worry, longing, etc., into three basic categories:

1. Ignorance, delusion, laziness, narrow-mindedness, and similar emotions.
2. Desire, clinging, longing, and such.
3. Aversion, aggression, hatred, dislike, fear, and such.

Sometimes these are spoken of as the Five Poisons, with the fourth and fifth categories under the third category, anger/aversion. The fourth is pride, inflation, and such; and the fifth is jealousy, competitiveness, and such. They are often subsumed under the third category because they are considered to be forms or subsets of anger/aversion.

Three Yanas: *See* Theravada, Mahayana, Vajrayana.

Tonglen (Tibetan; "Sending and Receiving"): A compassion practice in which one breathes in the suffering of others and breathes out toward them one's wishes for their happiness.

Tulku [TOOL-koo] (Tibetan; "Emanation Body." Sanskrit: *Nirmanakaya*): An individual who has mastered their mind enough that they can control their landing in their next incarnation. The tulku system has been used in Tibet for heads of monasteries and sub-lineages to allow them to shoulder their responsibilities for many lifetimes. This is why His Holiness the Dalai Lama XIV is referred to as the fourteenth: he has been recognized and has held the Office of the Dalai Lama thirteen previous times.

Two Truths (Tibetan: *denba nyi*): The two aspects of reality, like two sides of one coin. These two aspects are called Relative Truth (*kün dzop denba*) and Absolute Truth, or Ultimate Truth (*dön-dam denba*).

Vajrayana: A branch of Mahayana, which uses many skillful means from the tantras to pursue enlightenment more efficiently. It is the branch of Buddhism generally practiced by Tibetans.

Vipassana (Tibetan: *Lhaktong*; "Sublime Insight"): Usually practiced along with Shamata/Shiney. The practice of seeing the true nature of either the object of our attention or us ourselves.

Wang, Lung: These are two kinds of transmissions that a lama gives to students, to connect and open their minds in a profound way to a particular cycle of teachings and/or practices.

Yeshe: Also called timeless awareness or (primordial) wisdom. The wisdom inherent in the Dharmakaya, which shines forth into all of its created emanations.

Appendix B: Recommended Reading

FOR PRACTICE & GENERAL READING

David R. Loy. *The World Is Made of Stories*. Boston: Wisdom Publications, 2010. In this pithy book, Loy poetically shows us JUST how much our experience is a movie of our own making.

Dacher Keltner, Jason Marsh, and Jeremy Adam Smith. *The Compassionate Instinct*. New York: W. W. Norton & Company, 2010. Through stories and studies, the authors reveal the Buddha Nature in us all, ready to come forth at any time, often at surprising times.

Stephen Post, PhD, and Jill Neimark. *Why Good Things Happen to Good People*. New York: Broadway Books, 2008. This scientifically grounded book is an accessible, enjoyable read. Inspiring. The main study they refer to is a longitudinal study that involves in-depth annual interviews of the subjects over their entire adult lives.

Anam Thubten. *No Self, No Problem*. Point Richmond, CA: Dharmata Press, 2006. This is a great little book written by a true lama, but very accessible to a Westerner. It's pithy and full of gems that guide our minds in the direction we'd like them to go. He teaches Shamata regularly.

Any book by Mingyur Rinpoche. He also teaches Shamata regularly, as do an increasing number of his advanced, highly qualified students. They teach Ngöndro and other practices too. You can check all of this out on his website, www.tergar.org.

Michael Talbot. *The Holographic Universe*. Reprint edition. New York: Harper Perennial, 2011. I've said enough about this one for you to know it's packed with one thing after another that can really alter your viewing lens, so once again I recommend you take it in sips.

Daniel Siegel. *The Mindful Brain: Reflection and Attunement in the Cultivation of Well-Being*. New York: W. W. Norton & Company, 2007. This one you'd also want to take in sips. By the end you'll have a whole different understanding of your mind and your brain—more full and more detailed, but most important, more true.

Rick Hanson, PhD, with Richard Mendius, MD. *Buddha's Brain: The Practical Neuroscience of Happiness, Love, and Wisdom*. Oakland, CA: New Harbinger Publications, 2009. This is my favorite book on brain science in relationship to Buddhist meditation techniques. It really gets into the parts of the brain, what they do, how they work together, how that relates to how we feel, and how Buddhist methods can help us to use the brain in a way that allows us to practice equanimity while still feeling fully alive.

THREE BOOKS BY THUBTEN CHODRON

Buddhism for Beginners. Ithaca, NY: Snow Lion Publications, 2001.

Don't Believe Everything You Think: Living with Wisdom and Compassion. Ithaca, NY: Snow Lion Publications, 2013.

Working with Anger. Ithaca, NY: Snow Lion Publications, 2001.

Thubten Chodron is a Western Buddhist nun who speaks in a very down-to-earth way about the principles of Buddhism. Because she has applied these principles in her own life, she does a beautiful job of helping us apply them in our own.

BRAIN SCIENCE

Richard J. Davidson, PhD, with Sharon Begley. *The Emotional Life of Your Brain: How Its Unique Patterns Affect the Way You Think, Feel, and Live—and How You Can Change Them.* Reprint edition. New York: Plume, 2013. A long subtitle, but truly descriptive. Dr. Davidson is among the top neuroscientists in the growing field of Contemplative Science, which studies the effects of meditation on the brain, with full scientific rigor. He works closely with His Holiness the Dalai Lama. Given Dr. Davidson's accomplishments, we might expect to not be able to understand a thing—so it's a pleasant surprise to discover how readable and accessible this book is. Not one to leave it as an academic study, he has practiced meditation for many years. He is a living poster child of how richly we can cultivate positive habits of mind.

Daniel Goleman and Richard J. Davidson. *Altered Traits: Science Reveals How Meditation Changes Your Mind, Brain, and Body.* Paperback edition. New York: Penguin Random House, 2018. Though full of fascinating science tidbits, this is surprisingly readable because of the stories, as well as discussion of how the knowledge can be applied in our lives and ourselves.

ON COSMOLOGY

His Holiness the Dalai Lama. *The Universe in a Single Atom: The Convergence of Science and Sprituality.* New York: Morgan Road Books, Random House, 2005. This emerged from one of the Mind and Life meetings between prominent scientists and His Holiness the Dalai Lama. The subject of this one was cosmology. Appropriately enough for a conference on cosmology, this is a vast subject, with many scientific points of view, not all of which could be represented at that meeting. (There's information on the Mind and Life group's website in the "Websites" section below.) This book isn't an easy read, but a fascinating and historic one!

FUN & INSPIRING READING

Anna M. Cox. *Just As the Breeze Blows Through Moonlight: The Spiritual Life Journey of Thupten Heruka, a 19th C. Tibetan Yogi.* Bloomington, IN: Xlibris, 2002. This story—both an outer and inner adventure, set in old Tibet—came to Cox after she had been a practitioner for a long time. I didn't want to put it down. I was sad when it was over and I had to leave that world. One of those rare indulgences that's good for you.

Vicki Mackenzie. *Cave in the Snow: Tenzin Palmo's Quest for Enlightenment.* New York: Bloomsbury Publishing, 1998. This is the life story of an Englishwoman who found her way to great Tibetan masters in India, then spent twelve years practicing in a cave in Lhadak. She's come back to tell us about it. Very readable and inspiring.

Ani Tenzin Palmo. *Reflections on a Mountain Lake: Teachings on Practical Buddhism.* Ithaca, NY: Snow Lion Publications, 2002. This is Ani (nun) Tenzin Palmo's own book. It's full of advice and inspiration that's lovely to take in—in sips—and savor.

WEBSITES

Well, of course, there's ours: **namchak.org**. We have a lot of free teachings there, including online courses, opportunities to connect with others in your area and beyond, a little Sangha store, and more. You'll recognize some of the contents of this book, and audio or video support for some of its content. Other articles and teachings come and go too. We also have a large and growing library of print, audio, and visual teachings from our own lamas.

A fun and intriguing one is **spaceandmotion.com**. It combines a lot of different areas of knowledge, including histories of science and various branches of philosophy. My one caveat is that the website includes what I consider some questionable "science." The scientists represented there are respected by many, though considered controversial by some. But then, so was Galileo, in his time. If you liked *The Holographic Universe*, you'll be interested in this website.

Anam Thubten's website: **dharmata.org**.

Mingyur Rinpoche's website: **tergar.org**.

The Mind and Life group's website (**mindandlife.org**) offers a lot of historical and current thought on cosmology, with the goal of seeing how current scientific thought on the subject fits with Buddhist cosmology.

Dr. Richard J. Davidson's website: **centerhealthyminds.org**. This is one of my favorite brain science websites. They are doing cutting-edge research on such fascinating topics as the measurable effects of meditation on DNA, classroom behavior improvement through meditation, and measurably positive effects on military veterans who practice meditation.

Greater Good Science Center: **ggsc.berkeley.edu**. This is probably my very favorite one. It's FULL of simple and meaningful articles that really apply the science to life and vice versa. It also has the solid science for those who want to go down the rabbit hole more.

Appendix C: Credits & Permissions

This page is a continuation of the copyright page. Grateful acknowledgment is made for permission granted to reproduce images and to use quotes in the text.

PHOTOS & IMAGES

PAGES iii, iv, x, xii, xiv, xvii, xviii, xxii, 56–60, 77, 84–85, 98–101, 108, 112, 134, 135, 136: From *The Encyclopedia of Tibetan Symbols and Motifs* by Robert Beer, © 1991 by Robert Beer. Reprinted by arrangement with Shambhala Publications, Inc., Boulder, CO. www.shambhala.com.

PAGE ix: © 1998 Lama Tsomo LLC.

PAGE xi: © 2017 Namchak LLC, photo courtesy of Keegan Connell.

PAGE xii: © 2014 Lama Tsomo LLC.

PAGE xiv: Brenda Ahearn photo. © 2010 Daily Inter Lake. Reprinted with permission of Daily Inter Lake. No unauthorized use permitted.

PAGES xx–xxi, 11, 32-33, 44, 61, 66, 78, 94: Photos © 2006 Alison Wright; PAGE xix: Photo © 2007 Alison Wright; PAGES xxiv, 1, 62: Photos © 2010 Alison Wright; PAGE 10: Photo © 2011 Alison Wright.

PAGES xxiii, 4–5, 7, 14-15, 24, 26–27, 29, 30, 35, 43, 47, 54–55, 87, 93, 110–111, 113, 131: Photos © 2012 Radd Icenoggle.

PAGES 38, 39, 51: Photos © 2013 Sprout Films, Inc.

PAGES 42, 90: Photos © 2014 Rosemary Pritzker.

PAGE 45: Attribution unkown.

PAGES 56, 58, 59, 60: From Dr. Masaru Emoto © Masaru Emoto, LLC. Reprinted by arrangement with Office Masaru Emoto. http://www.masaru-emoto.net

PAGES 82, 83: Photos © 2012 The Camera Girls. Reprinted with permission of The Camera Girls. No unauthorized use permitted.

PAGE 98: University of Pennsylvania Archives.

PAGE 99: Photo of David Bohm. Keystone/Hulton Archives/Getty Images.

PAGE 103: Photo of Carl Jung. Demitri Kessel/The Life Picture Collection/Getty Images.

BOOKMARK: Image of Buddha. Buddha Shakyamuni III © 2019 Images of Enlightenment. Reprinted by arrangement with Dakini As Art. www.dakiniasart.org. Used with permission.

QUOTES

PAGE 63: "Human Touch" by Bruce Springsteen. Copyright © 1992 Bruce Springsteen (ASCAP). Reprinted by permission. International copyright secured. All rights reserved.

PAGE 93: From *What Is the Sangha? The Nature of Spiritual Community* by Sangharakshita © 2000, p. 36. Reprinted by arrangement with Windhorse Publications, Ltd., Cambridge, England, www.windhorsepublications.com.

PAGE 97–98: From *The Firmament of Time* by Loren Eiseley. Copyright © 1960 by Loren Eiseley; copyright renewed © 1988 by John A. Eichman, III. Reprinted with permission of Scribner, a division of Simon & Schuster, Inc. All rights reserved.

PAGES 99–100: Fred Pruyn, Aug/Sept 1997 issue *Sunrise Magazine*, "Infinite Potential: The Life and Times of David Bohm." Used by permission from Theosophical University Press.

PAGE 100: David Bohm, "Hidden Variables and the Implicate Order," in *Quantum Implications: Essays in Honour of David Bohm*, eds. Basil J. Hiley and F. David Peat, p.40. Copyright © 1987 by Hiley and Peat. Reprinted by arrangement with Routledge & Kegan Paul, London.

PAGES 101: For English language print rights: Excerpts from pp. 46, 47 from *The Holographic Universe* by Michael Talbot. Copyright © 1991 by Michael Talbot. Reprinted by permission of HarperCollins Publishers. For e-Book and audio digital download rights in English, Chinese and Tibetan: "The Holographic Universe" by Michael Talbot. Copyright © 1991. Reprinted by arrangement with The Barbara Hogenson Agency, Inc. All rights reserved.

Index

A

Absolute Truth, 75–76
Akshobhya, 104
Amitabha, 104
Amogasiddhi, 104
Anam Thubten Rinpoche, 73
archetypes, fundamental, 3, 104. *see also*
    Five Yeshes; images, archetypal
awareness: Yeshe as, 104–106. *see also* Five
    Dhyani Buddhas; *see also* emptiness/
    awareness

B

Bhikkhu Bodhi, 73
Bodhicitta, 31, 34; defined, 34n
Bohm, David, 99–101, 102, 105, 107
brain function: how practice alters, 7, 69;
    in imagined experience, 108
Buddha. *See* Buddha Shakyamuni; Five
    Dhyani Buddhas; Three Jewels
Buddha Mind, 54–55
Buddha Nature, 31, 34, 109; as true
    nature, 73, 95–97, 111
Buddha Shakyamuni: attains
    enlightenment, 67; compassion of, 62,
    92; discovers suffering, 63–65; early life
    of, 62–63; seeks enlightenment, 65, 68;
    as teacher, 67, 68, 92
Buddhafield, 77, 106

C

Chökyi Nyima, 28, 34, 36, 37, 40
compassion, 25, 68, 92, 104; of Buddha,
    62, 92; of Dalai Lama, xix–xxi; practice
    develops, 23; reality as, xxi, 80, 97, 105;
    of Tibetans, 2, 91; of Tulku Sangak,
    51–52; *see also* Bodhicitta; Buddha
    Nature
cultural influences on Western Buddhists,
    30–31
Cultural Revolution, 48–53

D

daily practice, 5
Dalai Lama XIV, His Holiness, 25;
    compassion of, xix–xxi; eats meat, 28;
    foreword by, xiii; happiness of, 91;
    as head of Gelugpa Lineage, 53; on
    karma, 90

Damtsik Drölma, 106
daughter, author's, 40, 86–87
deities. *See* archetypes, fundamental;
    Five Yeshes; images, archetypal;
    Sambhogakaya; *specific names of
    individual deities*
delusion, 81, 92
Dharma: Buddha teaches, 67; meanings
    of, 73–74; *see also* Three Jewels
Dharmakaya, 102, 103, 104
Dilgo Khyentse Rinpoche, 53, 69
Dönyöd Drupa, 106
Dzigar Kongtrül Rinpoche, 46–47
Dzogchen, 28, 29, 37–41, 53

E

Earth Changes, 16
ego identification: causes suffering, 52, 72,
    80–81, 86, 91–93; giving up, 92, 96
Eightfold Noble Path, 73–74
Einstein, Albert, theories of, 9, 13, 99
Eiseley, Loren, 97–98
Emoto, Masaru, 56, 57, 59
empowerments, 24, 41, 53
emptiness/awareness, 70, 89; author
    experiences, 17–18, 42, 43; as Buddha
    Nature, 95–98. *see also* Buddha Nature;
    as Dharmakaya, 102, 103. *see also*
    Dharmakaya; ego identification vs., 80;
    Relative Truth vs., 76; *see also* awareness;
    reality
enlightenment: Buddha motivated to
    attain, 62–68; as process, 42, 96; *see also*
    Four Noble Truths; Three Jewels; Three
    Kayas; Two Purposes
epiphanies, author's, 17–19, 23, 40, 42, 43
Ewam: meaning of, 41; as nonprofit, 41

F

faith, blind, 67; inquiry vs., 6. *see also*
    questioning
father, author's, 11, 13, 14, 17, 84–85
Five Dhyani Buddhas, 104–108. *see also*
    specific names of individual Buddhas
Five Yeshes, 104–106. *see also* Five Dhyani
    Buddhas; *specific names of individual
    Yeshes*
Four Noble Truths, 69–74
freedom, xxi
Freud, Sigmund, 16

123

Lama Sangak Yeshe Tsomo

CURRICULUM VITAE

Education & Professional Training

2006–present: One to two months' retreat annually, with instruction and guidance from Tulku Sangak Rinpoche and Khen Rinpoche.

1995–present: Scores of teachings, empowerments, and pilgrimages, including the following:

- One-week and two-week Dark retreat instruction retreats with Tulku Sangak Rinpoche and Khen Rinpoche (2017–present).
- Semiannual ten-day Dzogchen instruction retreats with Tulku Sangak Rinpoche (2006–2010).
- Six years of ten-day instruction retreats on *The Treasury of Precious Qualities*, a classic text that includes the entire Buddhist path. Tulku Sangak Rinpoche, Khen Rinpoche, and Anam Thubten Rinpoche, instructors.
- Finished Ngöndro (Preliminary Practices). This involved 108,000 prostrations; 108,000 repetitions of the 100-Syllable Mantra; 1,200,000 recitations of the Vajra Guru Mantra; and other similarly extensive practices.
- Small-group meeting with His Holiness the Dalai Lama. Ann Arbor, Michigan (April 2008).
- Tenshuk offering to His Holiness the Dalai Lama. Dharamsala, India (as part of a ten-day pilgrimage, July 2007).
- Two interviews with His Holiness the Dalai Lama.

2005 in Nepal and 2006 in the US: Lama ordination (bestowed by Tulku Sangak Rinpoche).

1995–2005: Ongoing intensive lama training in the Nyingma tradition, with Rinpoche. The following were among the components of the training:

- Thirty 1- to 2-week training intensives.
- Traditional three-year retreat, in strict, solitary retreat conditions, under Rinpoche's direct supervision, progressing from one stage of training to the next, finishing with the highest levels of Dzogchen practice. The practice retreats were usually done three months at a time.
- Several months of study and training at Rinpoche's monastery in Nepal.
- Ongoing scholarly and spiritual study of numerous classic Vajrayana Buddhist texts.
- Increased responsibility as a teacher under Rinpoche's guidance.
- Learned to speak fluent Tibetan, allowing ability to chant in Tibetan while understanding the meaning, to act as translator for students and practitioners, and perhaps most important, to speak extensively with Rinpoche and Khen Rinpoche, as well as other lamas, about the Dharma.

1990: MA, Counseling Psychology, Antioch University (emphasis: Jungian studies).

1987: BA, Counseling Psychology, Antioch University.

Affiliations & Memberships

Namchak Foundation, Montana. Co-founder, current board member.

Academy for the Love of Learning, Santa Fe, New Mexico. Founding Board member.

Ewam (US and international nonprofit center and school). Founding board member, board member, 1999–2004.

Light of Berotsana translation group, Boulder, Colorado. Board member, 2002–2008.

Namchak Foundation (US and international group with physical and online presence, dedicated to supporting people of the Namchak Lineage in Tibet and developing retreat sites). Co-founder with Namchak Dorlop Dorje Lopön Choeji Lodoe.

Pleasant Ridge Waldorf School, Viroqua, Wisconsin. Founder and board member, ca. 1975.

Selected Publications

The Dharma of Dogs: Our Best Friends as Spiritual Teachers, edited by Tami Simon. Sounds True, 2017. "Lama Kusung," pp. 33–35.

Why Is the Dalai Lama Always Smiling? (the earlier incarnation of this book and Book 2: *Wisdom & Compassion*). Namchak Publishing, 2016.

The Lotus & The Rose: Conversations Between Tibetan Buddhism and Mystical Christianity, with the Reverend Dr. Matthew Fox. Namchak Publishing, 2018.

"Ani Tsering Wangmo: A Life of Merit" in *Lion's Roar Newsletter*, March 2010.

"Coming Home" in *Originally Blessed*. Creation Spirituality Communities, 2008.

"Dharmasala" in *Lion's Roar Newsletter*, August 2007.

"Shedra" in *Lion's Roar Newsletter*, February 2006.

Selected Presentations & Teachings

"Expanding Capacities for Joy and Connection: Science and Practice," plenary session with Richard Davidson, PhD, and Lama Tsomo, Greater Good Science Center "Science of Happiness" Conference.

A variety of teachings, including weekly and short retreats (2005–present) when on-site at the Ewam center and at other US and international sites, including the New School in New York, Spirit Rock in California, East Bay Meditation Center, etc.

"Building the 'We' Economy from the Inside Out," COCAP 2019. Solo talk on compassion, then plenary session with Angel Kyodo Williams, Reverend Deborah Johnson, Konda Mason, and others.

Book launch events for *The Lotus and The Rose*, including "An Evening with Lama Tsomo and Matthew Fox," Sacred Stream, Berkeley, California; "East Meets West at Grace Cathedral," San Francisco.

Book launch events for *Why Is the Dalai Lama Always Smiling?* including "A Conversation with Van Jones," New York City; "A Conversation with Lama Tsomo and Sharon Salzberg," New York City; "Google Talks with Lama Tsomo," Mountain View, California.

Multiple co-presentations, including weekend retreats/workshops with Aaron Stern, founder of the Academy for the Love of Learning, and with Khen Rinpoche.

Three-hour introduction to Tibetan Buddhism, shown on TV in Taiwan. This was posted on YouTube in five installments.

Two guest appearances at the University of Montana School of Social Work. 2011.

"Once Existing from Self, Your Life Target Will Come Out Like Art Creation" (presentation to educators, students, artists, and general public). Miaolie Pottery. Miaolie, Taiwan. May 2010.

"Solving Confusion in the Mind" (presentation to Taiwan Sunshine Women's Association). Taichung Ewam Centre. Taichung, Taiwan. May 2010.

"Experience Sharing: To Change Your Life and Career from Miserable to Successful by Learning the Methods of Mind Observation Training" (talk to twenty-five business owners and senior managers). Howard Hotel. Taipei, Taiwan. April 2010.

"Learning Buddhism" retreat. Taichung Ewam Centre. Taichung, Taiwan. April 2010.

"Learning Buddhism and Doing Practices to Clarify Confusion." Howard Hotel. Taipei, Taiwan. April 2010.

"Seven Point Mind Training." Yung Ho Training Centre. Taiwan. March 2010.

"Seven Point Mind Training, 3rd Installment," retreat. Ewam. Arlee, Montana. November 2009.

"Inner Peace/Outer Peace: What Is the Relationship?" (with Frances Moore Lappé). Peace Festival. Ewam. Arlee, Montana. September 2009.

"Seven Point Mind Training, 2nd Installment," retreat. Ewam. Arlee, Montana. May 2009.

"Seven Point Mind Training, 1st Installment," retreat. Ewam. Arlee, Montana. April 2009.

"Organic Food and Buddhism" (presentation to second-level Buddhists). Howard Hotel. Taipei, Taiwan. March 2009.

"Enjoy Your Life with Happiness" and "From Common Happiness to Common Bodhi." Taipei Shilin Resort. Taipei, Taiwan. March 2009.

"Gratitude; Visualization; Dreams Come True, as Your Wishes." National Normal University. Taipei, Taiwan. March 2009.

Ngöndro retreat. Ewam Center. Hong Kong. November 2008.

"Buddhism." Unitarian Universalist Church. Missoula, Montana. May 2008.

"How to Make Your Mind Happy" (seminar). National Normal University. Taipei, Taiwan. March 2008.

"Keep Your Soul and Spirit in Good Health—Removing Torments and Mastering Your Spirit." Taichung County Cultural Center. Taichung, Taiwan. March 2008.

"Skillful Means Using Dharma to Benefit Others in Our Daily Lives." Ewam Center. Hong Kong. March 2008.

"Interaction and Modification of the Buddha Dharma Internal Spirit." Haufan University. Taipei, Taiwan. March 2008.

"Transforming Inner and Outer Worlds: Christian Mysticism and Tibetan Buddhism" (presentation with the Reverend Dr. Matthew Fox). Jung Center of Houston. February 2008.

"East Meets West: Christian Mysticism and Tibetan Buddhism" (presentation with the Reverend Dr. Matthew Fox). Stanford University Continuing Studies. Palo Alto, California. June 2007.

"Skills to Face Suffering" (Tonglen or Tranquil Abiding presentation to cancer patients). Tuen Mun Hospital. Hong Kong. January 2007.

"A Journey to a Peaceful Mind" (presentation to social workers and clients). City Hall Conference Room. Hong Kong. January 2007.

"How to Handle Suffering" (presentation to nursing staff). Tuen Mun Hospital. Hong Kong. January 2007.

"The Lotus and the Cross/The Lotus and the Rose" (invitation-only dialogue with the Reverend Dr. Matthew Fox). Academy for the Love of Learning. Location: Upaya Zen Center. Santa Fe, New Mexico. November 2006.

Series of interviews and presentations on Life TV, Taiwan (a 24-hour nationwide TV station devoted to Buddhist teachings). Topics included "The Pursuit of Happiness" (part of Woman Psychology Seminars). December 2006.

"Introduction to Buddhism and Buddhist Practice" (thirty-hour intensive course). University of Creation Spirituality. San Francisco, California. 2005.

Buddhist retreat (leader) on Ngöndro. Academy for the Love of Learning. Santa Fe, New Mexico. Location: Upaya Zen Center. Santa Fe, New Mexico. May 2005.

Khen Rinpoche

eAcknowledgments

It seems only right to begin with my family. My parents permanently infected me with the joy of exploring the nature of reality and understanding people. During my growing-up years, my sister sat with me for hours as we passionately replicated that pursuit. She's the real writer in the family, not to mention a brilliant editor, and she's always graciously encouraged my efforts.

I also want to thank Herman Schaalman, my family's rabbi, who gave me my first guidance and pointed me in the right direction in my pursuit of wisdom.

Four more whom I wish to acknowledge are my dogs Gonpo, Soongma, Kusung, and Dawa, my loving companions over the many years of writing this book . . . well, except for one writing stint at the monastery in Nepal. I deeply regretted that they were too big to fit in my carry-on bag.

I'm a teacher, and this series is a succession of many teachings. If it weren't for all of the students over the years and decades, I would not know what or how to teach. If it weren't for students' needs calling this forth from me, I wouldn't have troubled myself to write it. If it weren't for future students, I certainly wouldn't have written it. For all of this, and such inspiring open-minded and open-heartedness, I'm deeply grateful.

I feel a great deal of gratitude for my editor, Michael Frisbie, who is not only top-notch at the art of editing, but a natural and accomplished educator. Given that this was my first real attempt at a full-length book, I needed both of those gifts in great measure. Had it not been for him, this book would have been just a nice manual. That is what I'd originally had in mind. But because of his genuine enthusiasm for the material (despite not being a Buddhist) and his skills, his questions and comments evoked the rest of this book, which was actually in there somewhere. He always gave generously, and with good humor. Actually a hysterical sense of humor!

Huge thanks to Mary Ann Casler for her lovely work on the design, layout, and images for the original version of this book, which was titled *Why Is the Dalai Lama Always Smiling?* She guided us expertly through the galley and print process, as well as myriad details involved in publishing a book. For the beautiful layout and design of this new volume, applause to Kate Basart, who is not only skillful but a pleasure to work with. Thanks to Erin Cusick for her care and skill in proofreading, and to Colleen Kane from Namchak Publishing, for holding the many threads that wove together for the final product. Many thanks to Merry Sun for her excellent editing with a Millennial take; I would have no idea!

Much gratitude to the entire Namchak team, who contributed to the many aspects of putting a book together and sending it off into the world. I'm especially thinking of Keegan in IT, for wrestling Word to the ground repeatedly, and to Mitch, for jumping in as needed. Much gratitude to Jessica Larson, director of Education and Outreach, for her many key roles in bringing this out into the world. A few people supported in their consulting roles, with great skill and genuine enthusiasm: Jenny Best, Liz Koch, and especially Anne Tillery, founder of Pyramid Communications.

Many thanks to Janna Glasser, not only for her excellent tracking down of the shocking number of permissions for this book, but for the various legal agreements as well. But beyond that she is one of our more ardent supporters. Thanks to Jason Hicks, aided and abetted by Deborah Hicks, for recording the audio version of this entire book—no small feat! Gratitude to JoAnn Hogan for managing the countless details necessary for the success of this project.

Arthur Zajonc, emeritus professor of physics at Amherst and past president of Mind and Life Institute, was kind enough to read and comment on the physics tidbits. Dr. Richard Davidson, one of the neuroscientists in the Mind and Life Institute working with His Holiness the Dalai Lama xiv, and head of the Center for Healthy Minds and of the Waisman Center at the University of Wisconsin–Madison, took precious time from his busy schedule to talk to me and review my neuroscience pieces.

Lama Chönam and Sangye Khandro, co-founders of the Light of Berotsana translation group, read an early version of my manuscript and gave me lots of crucial feedback, corrections, and encouragement. Tulku (title meaning "reincarnated abbot") Anam Thubten Rinpoche, from whom I've been fortunate enough to receive teachings, read and gave me helpful comments and great encouragement on my nearly finished manuscript. Also in the Experts on Tibetan Buddhism camp was Namchak Dorlop (full name Namchak Dorje Lopön Choeji Lodoe), Tulku Sangak Rinpoche's brother, who reviewed the manuscript for accuracy.

As always, I'm deeply grateful for my co-conspirator in many things, beloved/adopted kin, and "witness to my life," Aaron Stern.

I feel these acknowledgments must include—and highlight—the masters of the Namchak Lineage, our particular branch of the larger Nyingma Lineage, beginning with Nup Sangye Yeshe, who hid the teachings, then Tsasum Lingpa, who later revealed those teachings, continuing in an unbroken thread of wisdom, down to the present world lineage holder, Tulku Sangak Rinpoche, to whom this book is dedicated. And my deep gratitude to Namchak Khen Rinpoche, Tulku Sangak Rinpoche's brother, who has also taught me much Dharma. Perhaps his greatest teaching is his living evidence of its efficacy. The most recent revealer of the teachings of our lineage was Pedgyal Lingpa, who passed them directly to Tulku Sangak Rinpoche. Without every one of the lineage lamas passing the wisdom down from one to the next with utmost care, I would not have received the gems that I talk about in this book. A lineage of teachings that is revealed and passed down in this way is referred to as a *treasure*. And that's actually an understatement.

I wouldn't want to receive all that Rinpoche and those who came before have offered me and not transmit what I can. Whenever I felt my lack of readiness too keenly, I also had this thought: if I had come upon this book when I was much younger, I know that I would have been delighted to use it as a beginning. If this book turns out to be of benefit to you, then my purpose for writing it will have been fulfilled.